Corporate Acquisitions and Mergers in Turkey

Corporate Acquisitions and Mergers in Turkey

Mert Elçin
Beliz Zorlu
Edmund Emre Ozer

This book was originally published as a chapter in Corporate Acquisitions and Mergers.

General Editor: Peter Begg

Wolters Kluwer

Published by:
Kluwer Law International B.V.
PO Box 316
2400 AH Alphen aan den Rijn
The Netherlands
E-mail: lrs-sales@wolterskluwer.com
Website: www.wolterskluwer.com/en/solutions/kluwerlawinternational

Sold and distributed by:
Wolters Kluwer Legal & Regulatory U.S.
920 Links Avenue
Landisville, PA 17538
United States of America
E-mail: customer.service@wolterskluwer.com

ISBN 978-94-035-2856-4

e-Book: ISBN 978-94-035-2986-8
web-PDF: ISBN 978-94-035-2996-7

Contents

KINSTELLAR

Kinstellar is an independent regional law firm in Emerging Europe and Central Asia, founded in 2008 as a spin-off of the Bratislava, Bucharest, Budapest and Prague offices of Linklaters. Since its foundation in 2008, Kinstellar has opened new offices in Istanbul (Turkey), Belgrade (Serbia), Bulgaria (Sofia), Almaty (Kazakhstan), Uzbekistan (Tashkent) and Croatia (Zagreb). Kinstellar advises leading global and local companies, financial institutions and governments on their most challenging transactions and assignments.

Kinstellar's Istanbul office was established in 2010 and is now recognized as one of the premier law firms in Turkey. In order to comply with Turkish Bar regulations, Kinstellar provides Turkish law advice through its affiliated Turkish attorney partnership, Gen Temizer Avukatlık Ortaklığı.

Authors

This chapter has been prepared and edited by Mert Elçin, Senior Associate, Beliz Zorlu, Associate and Edmund Emre Ozer, Partner.Kinstellar / Gen Temizer Avukatlık Ortaklığı

Levent Mah., Ebulula Mardin Cad. No: 55

34330, Besiktas / Istanbul Turkey

Tel.: +90 212 260 3400

E-mail: www.kinstellar.com

1 INTRODUCTION

1.1 General Introduction

1.1.1 Historical Background

[01] After seven centuries of Ottoman rule, the Republic of Turkey was established in 1923, in the wake of World War I. Today Turkey is considered to be a democratic, secular, unitary, constitutional republic with a diverse cultural heritage.

1.1.2 Geographical Location and Population

[02] Turkey shares borders with Bulgaria, Georgia, Greece, Armenia, Azerbaijan, Iraq and Syria. Its geographical location puts Turkey in an exceptional strategic position between Southeastern Europe and the Middle East. The capital of Turkey is Ankara. Turkey's population is over 82 million, comprised of diverse ethnic backgrounds, including Turks, Kurds and Armenians. The official language of the state is Turkish.

1.1.3 Membership of Trade Alliances and International Community

[03] Turkey is a member of the Council of Europe, NATO, OECD, OSCE and the G-20 major economies. After being an associate member of the European Economic Community since 1963 and joining the EU Customs Union in 1995, Turkey began full membership negotiations with the European Union in 2005. Turkey is a member of the Turkic Council, the Joint Administration of Turkic Arts and Culture, the Organisation of Islamic Cooperation and the Economic Cooperation Organization.

1.1.4 Economy

[04] Turkish markets have gradually opened up through economic reforms which mitigated the direct control of the government over foreign investments. Over the last thirty years, Turkey has witnessed the privatization of many of its publicly owned industries, such as energy and communications, and more recently, an increasing element of direct foreign investment is taking place in these and other important sectors.

[05] Turkey suffered from the global financial crises of 1994, 1999 and 2001. A new currency, the 'Turkish Lira' was launched in 2005 in order to balance the chronic high inflation. In the period between 2005 and 2017, the Turkish economy was one of the fastest-growing economies in the region and among the strongest in the world. Since 2018, Turkey has been experiencing a currency and debt crisis, caused by the Turkish Lira plunging in value and increased inflation. Given the Turkish economy's current account deficit and the private sector's large amounts of

foreign-currency-denominated debt, the devaluation of the currency and high inflation have resulted in a slowdown in economic growth. Nevertheless, the Turkish economy remains an 'open economy' with few restrictions on foreign inward investment and continues to attract investment both regionally and globally with a well-established infrastructure. It is home to a significant number of internationally active exporters and construction companies which generate significant foreign currency earnings and is rapidly establishing itself as a dynamic tech hub centred around Istanbul.

1.1.5 Legal Environment

[06] The Turkish legal system follows the continental European civil law tradition. After the establishment of the Turkish Republic in 1923, the legal system was modernized based largely on German and Swiss law.

[07] Since Turkey began accession negotiations with the European Union, there has been an extensive effort to harmonize national legislation with the EU *acquis communautaire* and to improve the administrative capacity for effective implementation of new laws and regulations.

1.1.6 Commercial Code

[08] The new Turkish Commercial Code (TCC) No. 6102 entered into force on 1 July 2012. The TCC governs most commercial transactions in Turkey. For transactions that are not governed by the TCC, the Turkish Code of Obligations (TCO) No. 6098 applies. The TCC and the TCO were renewed in 2012 as a part of an in-depth law reform exercise, taking the Swiss Code of Obligations Code as the basis and inspiration for the preparation of both the TCC and TCO. Broadly speaking, these primary sources of Turkish commercial legislation are harmonized with analogous European legislation.

1.1.7 Dispute Resolution

[09] Dispute resolution before the domestic courts typically take two to four years to be resolved. Consequently, foreign investors tend to choose arbitration for a dispute resolution. Arbitration in Turkey is regulated under the Code of Civil Procedure No. 6100 which entered into force on 1 October 2011 (CCP) and the Turkish International Arbitration Code No. 4686 which entered into force on 5 July 2001 (TIAC). Istanbul Arbitration Centre was established in 2015 under Istanbul Arbitration Centre Law No. 6570 with an arbitration centre located in Istanbul.

1.2 The Corporate Environment

1.2.1 Available Corporate Structures

[10] Business can be conducted in Turkey through a variety of different commercial entities, which include sole traders and companies. Commercial partnerships (*adi ortaklık*), joint-stock companies (*anonim şirket*), limited liability companies (*limited şirket*), unlimited liability companies (*kollektif şirket*), commandite companies (or limited partnerships) (*komandit şirket*) and cooperatives (*kooperatif*) are the types of companies regulated under the TCC. The last three are rarely preferred for regular businesses, especially by foreign investors. Foreign entities can also conduct business in Turkey via a branch or a liaison office whose activities are more limited than those of a company.

1.2.2 Commercial Register

[11] All companies except commercial partnerships are required to be registered with the Turkish Commercial Register. Registration is a condition of incorporation for a company. Registration with the Commercial Register normally takes not more than two to three weeks if all required documents are properly submitted and on time. These registration documents are:

(i) a company establishment petition and a notification form duly completed and signed by persons authorized to represent the company;
(ii) articles of association including notarized signatures of founders and notarial certification proving that all shares constituting the registered capital have been subscribed by the founders named in the articles of association;
(iii) a founders' statement signed by the founders;
(iv) a bank letter evidencing that the share capital has been deposited;
(v) a bank receipt indicating that 0.04% of the share capital of the company has been deposited to an account of the Turkish Competition Authority (TCA) at a state bank;
(vi) a permit or letter of compliance for companies whose incorporation is subject to the issuance of a permit or letter of compliance issued by the relevant ministry or other official institution;
(vii) a notarized copy of specimen signatures of persons who have the authority to represent and bind the company;
(viii) an application number indicating that the trade name to be used has been checked and confirmed by the Commercial Register;
(ix) a company establishment statement form;
(x) a certificate of residence of the company founders; and
(xi) a notarized translation of passport of foreign shareholders who are natural persons, or an apostilled and notarized translation of a registry document issued by the competent authority of the country of origin of foreign shareholders who are legal entities.

[12] The registration of the new information and amendments to the existing company information in the Commercial Register are of a declaratory nature. A third party may rely in good faith on the information received from the Commercial Register regarding a company. Various company information, including minutes of the ordinary and extraordinary general assembly meetings, minutes of the ordinary and extraordinary meetings of the board of directors, the articles of association, etc. must be published in the Turkish Commercial Register Gazette which is accessible over the internet on www.ticaretsicil.gov.tr. All documents to be submitted to the Commercial Register and the Commercial Register Gazette must be in the Turkish language.

1.2.3 Foreign Members of Executive Bodies

[13] A foreign natural or legal person can be a member of the board of directors of a joint-stock company and of a limited liability company.

1.3 Joint-Stock Company

1.3.1 Basic Characteristics

[14] A joint-stock company may carry out activities for any economic purpose unless forbidden by law. It can be incorporated by one person and there is no limit on the maximum number of shareholders. Shareholders can be foreign or Turkish natural persons or legal entities.

1.3.2 Founding

[15] Registration with the Commercial Register and tax office where the company is located is required for the incorporation of a joint-stock company. The articles of association must also be registered to the Commercial Register with the founding documents. There is no limit on the lifetime of a joint-stock company. A joint-stock company cannot be directly established by way of a public offer under Turkish law, but it can be established with a commitment to become a publicly traded company.

1.3.3 Registered Capital and Shares

[16] A joint-stock company's capital is determined and divided into shares. It must have a minimum capital of TL50 000 (approximately USD2 700) (or TL100 000 (approximately USD5 400) for closely held joint-stock companies which adopt the registered capital system) with a minimum nominal value of TL0.01 per share. The nominal value of the shares is stipulated by the articles of association. It is possible to issue shares with different nominal values.

[17] The shares may be either registered (in the name of a shareholder) or bearer shares. The articles of association can also provide multiple classes of shares and attach different rights to such classes of shares. The most common variations are in (i) dividend rights, (ii) liquidation rights and (iii) voting rights.

[18] Shareholders must pay (in full or in instalments) the amount of the shares that they have committed to subscribe to the share capital of the joint-stock company. If the shares are subscribed in cash, at least 25% of the share capital must be paid up before registration, and the remaining share capital needs to be paid within twenty-four months following the registration.

[19] All information regarding the share capital and the shares of a joint-stock company is recorded at the Commercial Register and published in the Commercial Register Gazette. The capital of joint-stock companies may be paid in cash or in kind. A joint-stock company can increase its capital by means of a resolution rendered by its general assembly.

[20] The TCC regulates the capital increase in registered capital system and introduces an important innovation concerning closely held joint-stock companies. Accordingly, in the event that the authority to increase the capital up to the authorized share capital is granted to the board of directors in a closely held joint-stock company, the board of directors is allowed to increase the capital within limits set forth by the general assembly, with no need for a general assembly resolution each time.

1.3.4 Acting on Behalf of a Joint-Stock Company

[21] A joint-stock company is represented, managed and bound by its board of directors consisting of one or more natural persons or legal entities. If a legal person becomes a member of the board, a natural person must be appointed to act on behalf of the legal person on the board. The number and the term of office of the board members are indicated in the articles of association. The term of office of the board members cannot exceed three years.

[22] The board of directors, being the executive body of a joint-stock company, is responsible for the internal management of the company, and it also represents the company vis-à-vis third parties. The board has the power to carry out all legal acts on behalf of the joint-stock company that are consistent with the objects of the company.

[23] The duties of the board of directors include (i) managing and representing the company; (ii) calling the general assembly for ordinary and extraordinary meetings; (iii) preparing the annual report for the activities of the company, balance sheet, profit/loss accounts; (iv) keeping the company books; (v) implementing the resolutions adopted by the general assembly.

[24] In principle, the board of directors is allowed to delegate some of its duties. However, high-level management of the company, determination of the management structure, regulation of accounting and financial supervision plan, nomination of directors and similar authorized persons, high-level supervision, book keeping, reporting and reporting of the bankruptcy situation to the court are among the duties of the board of directors which the TCC stipulates may not be delegated.

1.3.5 Other Corporate Bodies

[25] A joint-stock company has two mandatory corporate bodies: (i) the board of directors and (ii) the general assembly. The absence of one of these two bodies constitutes a cause for termination of the company.

[26] The auditor is independent and is not a body of the joint-stock company. Auditors are natural persons or legal entities which offer independent auditing services to the company on a contractual basis.

1.3.6 Shareholders' Rights

[27] The shareholders of a joint-stock company are entitled to equal rights, regardless of the portion of their shares.

[28] All shareholders are entitled to receive a dividend if the company produces a profit and the general assembly has declared a dividend. The right to receive dividends is an inalienable right of the shareholders.

[29] In principle, shareholders have preemptive rights in order to protect themselves against dilution in their shareholdings. These preemptive rights can be limited by a decision of at least 60% of the shareholders for a purpose that is for the benefit of the company, its growth strategy or for legal purposes such as becoming a publicly traded company or merging with another company. Preemptive rights cannot be limited to the benefit of or to the detriment of specific shareholders.

[30] Every shareholder is entitled to attend ordinary and extraordinary general assemblies, to vote during the general assemblies, to demand further information (which is provided to all shareholders) on the company during the general assemblies and demand private auditing if necessary.

[31] The Capital Markets Law, No. 6362 (CML) provides two further rights to the shareholders of the publicly traded companies. These are (i) the right to sell and (ii) the right to leave. The shareholder of a publicly traded company may put its shares to the company such shareholder took part in a general assembly meeting where an important agenda (such as a merger, demerger, transfer of assets or change of scope of activity of the company etc.) was deliberated and decided, and that shareholder recorded its disagreement with that proposal in the minutes of the meeting.

[32] Turkish law also affords certain specific rights to the minority shareholders of joint-stock companies (i.e., shareholders holding less than 10% of shares of a joint-stock company that is not publicly traded, and less than 5% in a publicly traded joint-stock company). These rights, which aim to keep the balance between minority and majority shareholders and avoid the abuse by majority shareholders of minority shareholders in the exercise of their rights and powers, include the rights to:

- be represented at the board of directors;
- demand a rightful termination of the company;

- not release the board members of their liabilities;
- nominate a member to the board of directors;
- demand private audit;
- demand the distribution of registered share certificates;
- convene the extraordinary general assembly; and
- demand the negotiation of the financial reports are special rights which are attributed solely to the minority shareholders.

1.3.7 Liability of Board Members

(i) General

[33] Members of the board may only be held liable if they wilfully or negligently breach an obligation imposed on them by law or the articles of association, and consequently, a loss is incurred by the company, its shareholders or creditors. Negligence must be attributable to such board members individually.

[34] The board members and third parties in charge of management have a duty of care to protect the company's interests with good faith, failure of which constitutes negligence. In determining the level of care, the courts take into account the level of care expected from a prudent manager.

[35] Under the TCC, where two or more board members are liable for a loss, each is jointly and severally liable with the others to the extent that the loss is attributable to him personally on account of his own fault and the circumstances. Board members will be held liable pro rata for their contribution to the loss on a case-by-case basis. Consequently, a non-negligent board member (for instance, a member who has objected to a board resolution, the implementation of which resulted in a loss) will not be liable whereas negligent members will be held liable pro rata to their contribution to the damage.

(ii) Liability of Board Members of a Subsidiary

[36] If a Turkish company's board of directors is instructed and directed by a company which owns 100% of its shares and voting rights ('Controlling Shareholder'), the board members of such subsidiary may avoid liability towards the subsidiary and its shareholder (but shall be liable towards to the creditors). This rule will apply regardless of whether the Controlling Shareholder is located in Turkey or abroad.

(iii) Specific Liability in Relation to Merger

[37] There is a specific liability regime with respect to mergers, which does not exclude the general liability provisions. The board members who execute or carry out wrongful, fraudulent or misleading documentation, undertakings, declarations and guarantees in relation to a merger or who negligently participate in such acts are legally liable for the resulting losses and may face imprisonment from one to three years (for more detail on mergers, *see* section 11.2 below).

1.3.8 Other Important Issues

[38] Joint-stock companies and limited liability companies have been regulated as capital companies with limited liability, however, both company types differ from each other in many aspects such as their capital amounts, liability of shareholders and directors for tax debts social security premiums. For instance, a limited liability company is not able to issue and offer its shares to public whereas a joint-stock company has this possibility.

[39] Furthermore, there are several sectors such as banking and insurance, in which the establishment of a joint-stock company is required. Moreover, a joint-stock company is also appropriate for corporate governance.

1.4 Limited Liability Company

1.4.1 Basic Characteristics

[40] A limited liability company may carry out activities for any economic purpose unless forbidden by law. It can be incorporated by one or more Turkish or foreign natural persons or legal entities and the maximum number of shareholders (known as partners) cannot exceed fifty. There is no mandatory limit on the lifetime of a limited liability company although it is possible to limit its lifetime to a specific period.

[41] The liability of the partners is limited to the capital that they have subscribed to pay and this liability is towards the company. However, the limited liability company is fully liable for the debts of the company with all its assets.

1.4.2 Foundation

[42] Registration with the Commercial Register and tax office where the company is located is required for the incorporation of the company. The incorporation process can generally be completed within two to three weeks of submission of all required documents to the Commercial Register.

[43] The articles of association of a limited liability company which contain the title and headquarters, the scope of activity, the form of notices, the capital, the identity of the founding partners and the shareholding structure, the privileged shares of the company (if any) and the names, titles, nationalities of the directors, must be registered with the Commercial Register.

1.4.3 Registered Capital

[44] A limited liability company must have a minimum share capital of TL10 000 (approximately USD540) with a minimum nominal value of TL25 for each share (approximately USD1.35). The capital can be in cash or in kind. The share capital must be paid within twenty-four months following the registration.

[45] The company can issue registered or bearer shares and grant certain privileges and preferences to certain groups of shares.

[46] In contrast to joint-stock companies, the authorized capital system is not permitted for limited liability companies, i.e., the directors of a limited liability company cannot increase the capital without a general assembly resolution.

1.4.4 Acting on Behalf of a Limited Liability Company

[47] All management and signing powers may be granted to one or more partners or to third parties. If no manager is appointed, a limited liability company is managed by all its partners. In any case, at least one partner must have the authority to manage and bind the company. If a limited liability company has more than one manager, one of them is appointed as chairman of the management board. If a manager is a legal person, a natural person must be appointed to act on behalf of that legal person. Managers can be either Turkish or foreign citizens.

[48] A manager may be appointed within the articles of association upon the incorporation of the company or afterwards by a resolution of the general assembly.

[49] Resolutions are adopted with the vote of the majority of the management board, however, in case of a deadlock, the president of the management board has the casting vote.

[50] In principle, the managers and other managing persons are not allowed to engage in activities that are in competition with the company, however, it can be agreed otherwise in the articles of association or by the approval of the partners.

1.4.5 Other Corporate Bodies

[51] A limited liability company has two statutory bodies: (i) the general assembly of partners and (ii) the management board (if there is more than one manager a management board must be formed).

1.4.6 Personal Liability of Partners and Managers

[52] Unlike the shareholders of a joint-stock company, the partners of a limited liability company are personally liable, in proportion to their shareholding, for the public debt (such as taxes, social security premiums) of a limited liability company, where such debts cannot be collected from the limited liability company.

[53] The managers of a limited liability company who have the authority to bind the limited liability company and have signature power are personally liable for all of the unpaid public debts of a limited liability company. Unlike partners, each manager of a limited liability company is responsible for all public debts which cannot be collected from the limited liability company.

2 REGULATORY FRAMEWORK

2.1 General Introduction

[54] There is no specific legislation which regulates M&A practice in all its aspects in Turkey. However, the general principles governing M&A transactions are found in several laws and codes, depending on the nature and business of the relevant companies, including:

- the TCC, as amended;
- the CML, as amended;
- the TOC, as amended;
- the Law on Protection of Competition No. 4054, as amended;
- the Labour Law No. 4857, as amended (*'Labour Law'*);
- the Banking Law No. 5411, as amended (*'Banking Law'*);
- the Regulation Regarding Mergers, Acquisitions and Transfer of Shares of Banks (by Banking Regulation and Supervision Agency);
- the Insurance Law No. 5684, as amended (*'Insurance Law'*);
- the Regulation Regarding Establishment and Working Principles of Insurance and Reassurance Companies published in the Official Gazette dated 24 August 2007 and numbered 26623, as amended; the Communiqué on Merger and Demergers (Serial II No. 232 of the Capital Markets Board); the Communiqué No. 2010/4 on Mergers and Acquisitions Requiring the Approval (by the TCA);
- the Capital Markets Board (CMB) Communiqué on the Material Events (Serial II No. 15.1) (*'Disclosure Communiqué'*);
- the CMB Tender Offer Communiqué (Serial II No. 26.1) (*'Tender Offer Communiqué'*);
- the Foreign Direct Investment Law No. 4875 ('FDI *Law*'), as amended;
- the Law on Title Deeds, No. 2644 (*'Title Deed Law'*), as amended;
- the Electricity Market Law, No. 6446, as amended (*'Electricity Market Law'*);
- the Electricity Market Licensing Regulation as amended;
- the Natural Gas Market Law, No. 4646, as amended;
- the LPG Market Law, No. 5307, as amended;
- the Corporate Tax Law, No. 5520, as amended.

2.2 Foreign Direct Investment Law

[55] The aim of the FDI Law is to (i) encourage foreign direct investment in Turkey; (ii) protect the investors; (iii) comply with international standards; and (iv) increase the volume of foreign direct investment through streamlined policies and procedures. The FDI Law, as a major security provider for foreign investors, is based on principles such as freedom to invest, national treatment, access to real estate, dispute settlement, and valuation of non-cash capital.

[56] The notification-based approach is adopted in FDI Law, rather than an approval-based one. Accordingly, in the event that a company is incorporated in Turkey with a foreign investor as a shareholder, the relevant trade registry offices shall send to the Ministry of Economy a copy of the form and petition for incorporation, articles of association and the list of shareholders. Where a foreign investor acquires shares in a Turkish company through a capital increase or share transfer, the relevant Turkish company must notify the Treasury, through an online platform (E-TUYS), submitting information on the foreign investor and its shareholding within one month of the date of the share transfer or share issuance. Moreover, a Turkish company with foreign shareholding will only be required to provide the Ministry of Treasury and Finance every year with information through E-TUYS such as its activities, direct shareholding and shareholding percentages. The provisions of the sectoral laws (such as the Banking Law, Insurance Law) are reserved and impose further requirements for companies which fall under the scope of such legislation.

2.3 Commercial Law Aspects

[57] Whether an investment is carried out by way of establishing a new entity or participating in an existing company, the TCC makes no distinction between a local and a foreign shareholder. Foreign and domestic shareholders enjoy the same rights and privileges, subject to any limitations stipulated in the articles of association of a company. A shareholders' agreement may be entered into and, provided there is some foreign element, the parties may designate foreign law as the governing law of the shareholders' agreement. Likewise, arbitration may be stipulated for the resolution of disputes.

2.4 Real Estate Restrictions for Foreigners

[58] There are certain restrictions with regard to real estate acquisitions by foreign investors that are set out in Title Deed Law.

2.4.1 Foreign Companies

[59] Foreign companies established according to the relevant laws of their countries of origin can acquire real estate and limited rights in rem in Turkey only within the provisions of special laws. These special laws are the Petroleum Market Law, No. 5015, the Law on Tourism Incentives, No. 2634 and the Industrial Areas Law, No. 4737. Foreign legal entities other than commercial companies (such as foundations, associations etc.) cannot acquire real estate in Turkey.

2.4.2 Turkish Companies with Foreign Shareholding

[60] Turkish companies with foreign shareholding can acquire real estate or limited rights in rem to carry out the business activity specified in their articles of association with the approval of the relevant governorship. A Turkish company with foreign shareholding is a Turkish company in which foreign individuals or foreign legal entities (each being a 'foreign investor') either:

(a) hold 50% or more of the share capital; or
(b) hold the right to appoint or release members of the board of directors.

[61] If the foreign investor(s) hold less than 50% share capital and do not have a right to appoint or release members of the board of directors of a Turkish entity, such Turkish entity is considered as a local entity.

2.5 Capital Markets Board Supervision

[62] The CMB is the regulatory authority that supervises companies listed on the Istanbul Stock Exchange (i.e., Borsa Istanbul), as well as securities, intermediaries and portfolio management companies in Turkey. The CMB regulations applicable to a takeover of a public company are summarized below.

2.5.1 Public Disclosure

[63] The Disclosure Communiqué aims to ensure the transparent, reliable, effective, stable and fair operation of the capital markets, by requiring the timely disclosure of correct and full information to investors. Pursuant to the Disclosure Communiqué, a distinction between 'insider information' and 'ongoing information' is made. Insider information means all information, events and processes which may have an influence on the decisions of investors or value of the capital markets instruments and which has not been disclosed publicly. Ongoing information is defined as all information, events and processes other than insider information.

[64] There is an obligation of public disclosure if the insider information is acquired by persons who (i) owns directly or indirectly 10% or more of the shares or voting rights of the issuer, or (ii) regardless of such threshold owns 10% or more of the shares granting board member appointment or nomination privileges. If the insider information is disclosed to third parties during the course of business by an issuer or a person acting on his behalf such information must also be disclosed to public by the issuer.

[65] If a direct or indirect shareholder's total share capital or voting rights in a listed company meet or exceed the thresholds of 5%, 10%, 15%, 20%, 25%, 33%, 50%, 67% or 95%, the shareholder must make a public disclose of such information.

[66] The CMB also published disclosure guidelines for capital market instrument issuers pursuant to the Disclosure Communiqué. Consistent with established CMB practice, the guidelines clarify the communiqué's relatively general disclosure requirements, providing illustrative examples. The Disclosure Guidelines provide that all third parties, including the issuer's advisers, must be under a statutory or contractual obligation of confidentiality until that information is disclosed publicly.

2.5.2 Mandatory Tender Offer

[67] The Tender Offer Communiqué which entered into force on 23 January 2014 sets out the principles and guidelines governing mandatory and voluntary tender offers applicable to shareholdings in publicly held companies (*see* section 9 for details on the Tender Offer Communiqué).

[68] According to the Tender Offer Communiqué:

(i) the direct or indirect acquisition of more than 50% of the voting rights or, regardless of such threshold, the direct or indirect acquisition of privileged shares which give their holder the right to nominate or appoint a simple majority of the board members or that results in a change in management control; or
(ii) any shift in management control resulting from a contractual arrangement between the shareholders, triggers the MTO requirement.

2.6 Banking Regulatory and Supervisory Authority Approval

[69] The regulatory authority supervising banks and other financial institutions in Turkey is the Banking Regulation and Supervision Agency (BRSA).

[70] Any transfer of shares resulting in the direct or indirect acquisition by one person of 10% (or more) of the issued shares of a bank is subject to BRSA approval. Likewise, if the direct or indirect shareholding ratio of a shareholder reaches and/or exceeds, or falls below the thresholds of 10%, 20%, 33% or 50% of the capital of a bank, a BRSA approval must be obtained.

[71] In order to obtain BRSA approval, the transferees must submit proof of compliance with the requirements of the Banking Law in relation to becoming a shareholder of a bank. Obtaining BRSA approval generally takes eight to twelve weeks, provided that all information and documentation regarding the new shareholder are submitted in full and in appropriate form to the BRSA. According to the Banking Law, the BRSA approval is subject to the payment of a fee corresponding to 1% of the nominal value of the transferred shares to the Saving Deposit Insurance Fund of the Republic of Turkey.

2.7 Energy Markets Regulation Authority's Approval

[72] The regulatory framework for the electricity sector is mainly governed by the Electricity Market Law and the secondary legislation issued by the Energy Markets Regulation Authority (EMRA) as an independent regulatory authority responsible for the regulation and supervision of the electricity market. Under the Electricity Market Law, there is no specific restriction on foreign ownership.

[73] Licences issued by the EMRA under the Electricity Market License Regulation, Petroleum Market Licence Regulation and Natural Gas Market License Regulation may not be transferred. The rights and obligations of a licensee under its license may be assigned to a third party if such third party is established by way of spin-off of the licensee or merger if EMRA approval is obtained. Mergers and acquisitions are considered to be an efficient way of transferring licences for this reason.

[74] Pursuant to the above-referenced licensing regulations:

(1) the direct or indirect acquisition by a natural person or a legal entity of shares that amount to more than 10% of the share capital of a license holder that is a legal person (5% for a publicly traded company); and
(2) share acquisitions that result in a change of control of the share capital of a license holder independently of the above-mentioned percentages.

[75] Each requires the prior approval of EMRA. Consequently, consent from EMRA must be obtained for the merger or acquisition prior to completion.

[76] In principle, these transactions are governed by the TCC, but there are additional requirements set forth by the energy market regulations such as the obligatory context of the merger agreement. A clearance of the Competition Authority may also be required if the applicable thresholds are reached or exceeded.

2.8 Mergers and Acquisitions of Insurance Companies

[77] Pursuant to the Regulation Regarding Establishment and Working Principles of Insurance and Reassurance Companies, the following transactions are subject to the approval of the Ministry of Treasury and Finance (the '*Treasury*'):

(1) transfer of shares resulting in (whether directly or indirectly) a shareholder exceeding or falling below the thresholds of 10%, 20%, 33% or 50% of the capital of an insurance company;
(2) granting or terminating usufruct right (such as voting rights, dividend) over the shares representing 10%, 20%, 33% or 50% of the share capital of an insurance company;
(3) transfer of privileged shares with the right of appointing members to the board of directors, irrespective of the thresholds stated above.

[78] Transfers of shares without Treasury approval must not be recorded in the share ledger; any recording made in the share ledger in breach of the foregoing restrictions is deemed to be null and void.

[79] The approval procedure is described in detail under the Regulation. These companies must apply to the Treasury with a copy of their articles of association, a resolution of their general assembly approving such restructuring, the merger or transfer agreement and a detailed report including the reasons for such restructuring and financial analysis of potential post-restructuring situation of the companies in order to obtain such permission.

[80] Such companies can also transfer their portfolios with the permission of the Treasury.

2.9 Anti-bribery Laws

[81] Bribery is sanctioned under the Turkish Criminal Code No. 5237. If a person directly or indirectly bribes a public official or a third party designated by the public official, in order for such public official to do, or not to do, his/her duty, that person and the public official are punishable by a term of imprisonment from four to twelve years.

[82] Foreign anti-bribery legislation, such as the US Foreign Corrupt Practices Act and the UK Bribery Act may well be relevant considerations for parties considering M&A transactions involving Turkish companies. While anti-bribery and corruption (ABAC) due diligence remains unusual in purely domestic M&A transactions, it is becoming a more common requirement in transborder acquisitions, particularly those involving parties with connections to jurisdictions with strong track records in prosecution of bribery of foreign public officials.

3 MOST COMMON ACQUISITION TRANSACTIONS

3.1 Common Transactions for the Acquisition of Turkish Companies

[83] The most common acquisition transactions are:

(1) the acquisition of shares in a joint-stock company or in a limited liability company;
(2) the acquisition of a company's assets; and
(3) the acquisition of a company's business or a part thereof.

[84] The parties are free to determine the rights and obligations of the acquisition agreement as they see fit, as long as the mandatory provisions of Turkish law are fulfilled. In addition, various procedural requirements apply to each of these acquisition methods. The type and number of procedural requirements that must be fulfilled in order to carry out the selected acquisition method should also be considered with respect to timing and indirect acquisition costs in particular.

[85] During negotiations, the parties may execute a letter of intent or a memorandum of understanding setting out certain terms of the transaction. Unless expressly stipulated therein, neither a letter of intent nor a memorandum of understanding constitutes a binding obligation of the parties to enter into the transaction agreement. However, under certain circumstances, a party could be liable for damages, if it unjustifiably terminated the negotiations.

[86] Exclusivity agreements are commonly used in acquisitions. Although there are cases where the parties sign an exclusivity agreement as a separate agreement, it is normally included as a provision in the letter of intent. Exclusivity provisions usually include a longstop date until which negotiations between the parties will continue, and say that until this date, the transferor party must not offer the target shares (or other rights) to third parties.

4 ACQUISITION OF SHARES IN A JOINT-STOCK COMPANY

4.1 Transfer of Shares

[87] The title to shares is transferred by virtue of a share purchase agreement (an SPA). Parties can also agree in writing on the date of the title transfer, which may be any date following the execution of the SPA and may be conditional on the fulfilment of various conditions precedent to the transfer.

[88] The articles of association of a joint-stock company may restrict, but not exclude, the transferability of registered shares. Registered shares are transferable by endorsement and delivery to the purchaser. The endorsement must identify the purchaser and contain the date of the transfer and signature of the seller. A transfer of registered shares is effective in relation to a joint-stock company only when the transfer is evidenced to the joint-stock company and recorded in the shareholders' register. The company has the right to refuse to register the transfer for reasons specified in the articles of association. If the transfer is refused by the company, the acquirer of shares does not acquire full ownership status and is prevented from exercising governance rights, such as the right to vote, until the registration is completed.

[89] Bearer shares are transferred by and at the moment of their delivery or at any later moment stipulated in the SPA which must be notified to the Central Registry Agency (*Merkezi Kayıt Kuruluşu*). Failure to notify will result in the transferee's inability to exercise its governance rights.

[90] Share transfers, which directly or indirectly result in the shares possessed in the capital of a company to exceed or drop below 5%, 10%, 20%, 25%, 33%, 50%, 67% and 100%, must be notified to the company whose shares are acquired or sold and such notification must also be registered before the competent trade registry. Failure to notify will result in the inability to exercise rights associated with the share, including the right to vote.

[91] The joint-stock company is the only form of investment vehicle in Turkey whose shares may be listed on a stock exchange and offered for sale to the general public.

4.2 Consequences of the Acquisition of Shares

[92] The acquisition of shares has, in particular, the following consequences:

(1) The buyer acquires a shareholding in the company with all its existing assets and liabilities, including current and contingent tax and environmental liabilities. This also applies to any liabilities not disclosed in the accounts or during the due diligence process.
(2) The buyer of shares listed for trading on thc Istanbul Stock Exchange will have various reporting duties regarding the number of shares held by the buyer and also by entities acting in concert with the buyer. Furthermore, it may, upon exceeding certain thresholds, be obliged to carry out an MTO (*see* section 9.1 below).
(3) The buyer acquires a shareholding in the company with all licences and permits issued to it. If the company has any such licences or permits, the acquisition may be subject to notification of or approvals from the relevant authorities.
(4) The buyer becomes liable to pay up any outstanding capital contribution related to the shares. The buyer, however, is not liable for any other liabilities of the joint-stock company.
(5) An approval by the boards or the general meeting of shareholders of the seller, buyer or target company may be required for the sale of shares pursuant to the articles of association or other corporate documents (such as the signature circular).
(6) Generally, either (i) the seller's (or the buyer's) corporate documents or (ii) the law governing their incorporation may require additional consents for an acquisition.

4.3 Issues to Be Considered in Share Deals

[93] The possible use of the assets of the acquired joint-stock company as security for financing the acquisition is limited if the transaction is regarded as the provision of 'financial assistance' by the target company (for details, *see* section 10.1.2).

[94] Although contracts binding on the target joint-stock company generally remain in force, the potential buyer should become aware of any possible termination clauses in such contracts entitling the counterparty to terminate the contract in the event of any change of control. Such termination clauses are, for e.g., common in financing arrangements.

[95] The buyer of less than 100% of the shares in a joint-stock company should verify: (i) the level of the various majority requirements for adopting decisions of the target joint-stock company's general meeting, so that it can plan the purchase of shares required to effectively control the joint-stock company, and (ii) the rights of the remaining minority shareholders. Some of these requirements are provided for directly by the TCC and some may be provided for in the articles of association.

[96] Companies' right to acquire and take security over their own shares are recognized in a limited manner under the TCC:

(i) the total nominal value of the repurchased or pledged shares shall not exceed one-tenth of the share capital or issued capital of the company;
(ii) the general assembly of shareholders shall adopt a resolution to authorize the board of directors in order to repurchase or pledge the company's own shares within the abovementioned limit;
(iii) the remaining net assets of the company following the deduction of the repurchased share price shall be at least the sum of the share capital or issued capital and the reserve funds not to be distributed according to the TCC and the articles of association;
(iv) the price of the shares to be acquired or accepted as security must be fully paid up.

[97] An SPA may also be governed by laws other than Turkish law as long as the mandatory provisions regarding the manner of transfer of the title to the shares are observed. Many foreign investors tend to have the laws of their jurisdiction governing the SPA.

[98] The purpose of the shareholders' agreement is to regulate the rights and the obligations of the shareholders following the M&A transactions and during the term of their shareholding. Since the articles of association of a company is a public document, the parties often aim to regulate some matters (such as representations of undertakings of the shareholders, contractual penalties, voting arrangements, voting rights and procedure, non-competition obligations) by executing a shareholder agreement.

5 ACQUISITION OF SHARES IN A LIMITED LIABILITY COMPANY

[99] Unless otherwise provided in the articles of association, shares of a limited liability company may be freely transferred at all times.

[100] The seller and the buyer must execute a share transfer agreement in writing before a notary public. If the share transfer agreement is not concluded in the form required by law, such transfer will be null and void and will not be binding on the company and the parties.

[101] The seller and/or the buyer must notify the limited liability company regarding the transfer of shares and request its approval. Share transfers must be approved by a general assembly of partners with a quorum representing a majority of votes present in the meeting. Unless otherwise provided in the articles of association, general assembly of partners may reject a share transfer without any reason.

[102] Managers are responsible for registering the transfer of shares with the Commercial Register within thirty days from the date of approval of the share transfer. Transfers of shares must be registered in the share ledger of the company.

6 ACQUISITION OF ASSETS

6.1 General

[103] In an asset purchase transaction, the assets (tangible and/or intangible) are transferred individually and each must be precisely specified in the transaction documentation. Liabilities do not transfer along with individual assets, unless a particular liability is transferred by operation of law (e.g., mortgage, pledge, easement, lease contracts). Individual liabilities may be fully transferred only with the creditor's consent.

[104] The transfer of individual assets must be distinguished from the transfer of an entire business or a part thereof. The sale of a business as an ongoing concern results in the transfer of all assets and liabilities belonging to a particular business or part of a business (*see* section 7).

6.2 Specification of Assets and Liabilities

[105] The exact specification of all the assets (both tangible and intangible) to be transferred is vital for the enforceability of the transfer agreement. Where large numbers of assets are to be transferred, the individual assets are usually listed in an annex to the transfer agreement. In addition, there may be an interim period between the signing of the agreement and completion and, therefore, it may be necessary to stipulate that the list of assets in the annex is subject to change in the normal course of business. A provision for the disclosure of the completion accounts would be the normal method of assessing and identifying the state of the assets upon completion.

[106] The same requirements for exact specification apply to all liabilities that are to be transferred, subject to the consent of creditors. The exact identification of liabilities requires, in particular, identification of the creditor and the legal cause giving rise to the liability and possibly also the subject matter of performance or the amount.

6.3 Legal Requirements for the Transfer of Assets and Liabilities

[107] Turkish law distinguishes between the legal grounds for the transfer, usually a transfer agreement, and the actual transfer of title, which in certain cases requires an additional act of the transferor or a third party (such as hand-over or registration in a public registry).

[108] Transfers of movable property, such as machinery, vehicles and physical stock, require actual delivery in addition to a legally binding transfer agreement in order for the title to pass to the purchaser, although the parties may agree in writing on a title transfer date preceding or following the date of the actual delivery. The transfer agreement as such does not need to be in writing, but written form is recommended. A transfer agreement for vehicles must be signed before a notary public.

[109] With respect to the sale of movable property, the TCO provides for a buyer acting in good faith to acquire good title to the property even if the seller did not own it.

[110] Title to immovable property (real estate) registered in the Real Estate Register passes only upon registration of the transfer in the Real Estate Register. A transfer agreement for immovable property must be signed before (i) the competent Real Estate Register or (ii) a notary public as of 1 January 2023 according to the recent amendments to the Notary Law enacted on 28 June 2022. Please note acquisition of an immovable property by a foreign-owned Turkish company will trigger a governorate permission process in which the applicant company must apply to the governorship where the immovable property is located prior to the acquisition of any interest in an immovable property.

[111] Receivables are transferred by an assignment agreement, which must be in writing. Unless agreed otherwise, the debtor's consent to the assignment is not required. Once the assignment is notified to the debtor by the assignor or proven by the assignee, the debtor is able to discharge itself of its obligation only by performing its obligations to the assignee and not to the assignor.

[112] The transfer of intellectual property rights may require registration in a public register (for e.g., trademarks and patents). A trademark transfer agreement must be signed before a notary public, and the agreement must be registered with the Turkish Patent Institute. A company's business name registered in the Commercial Register may not be transferred without a simultaneous transfer of the business to which it relates.

[113] Securities in certificated form require physical delivery and, in most cases, also an endorsement by the transferor.

[114] Licences granted under public law may generally not be transferred. Even if a licence has been issued for operating an appliance, the new operator will usually need to apply for a new licence from the relevant authority.

[115] Contracts may not be assigned unilaterally by one party, unless provided for in the contract. Replacing a party to a contract by a third party requires a multi-party agreement with all parties to the original contract.

[116] Liabilities may be transferred by a debtor only with the consent of the creditor. In the absence of such consent, the transferor remains the debtor and has only a contractual right against the transferee for compensation.

[117] Some liabilities pass by operation of law together with the assets to which they pertain, in particular, in rem rights (e.g., mortgage, pledge, easement, pre-emptive rights).

[118] If a significant portion of assets relating to certain business activities that will be newly carried out by the transferee of the assets is transferred, employees attributable to such assets may pass by operation of law to the transferee.

[119] Turkish law sets forth that in rem rights are subject to the laws of the jurisdiction where the property is located. Even if the transfer agreement is governed by laws of a foreign jurisdiction, the transfer of the ownership of the assets transferred thereunder, as well as all disputes arising in connection with such transfer, would be subject to Turkish law if the assets are located in Turkey at the time of transfer.

7 ACQUISITION OF A BUSINESS OR A PART THEREOF

[120] The whole or part of a business of a company can be transferred to a third party.

[121] In case the whole of the business is intended to be transferred, rights and obligations related to the business will be transferred automatically to the transferee (unless specifically excluded on terms), in which case, both the transferor and the transferee will continue to be jointly liable against the creditors for the obligations arising from the business for a period of two years. The transfer agreement must be in written form and is required to be registered with the Commercial Registry. The transferor shall be liable for the obligations of the business as of the date when he notified the creditors of the transfer of business or gave a public notice thereof by newspaper publication.

8 REPRESENTATIONS AND WARRANTIES UNDER TURKISH LAW

[122] The concept of representations and warranties, as observed by English law, is not fully applicable under Turkish law. The purpose of representations is to provide the party in whose favour the representations are made with reasonable assurance that it may rely on certain facts when considering its intention to enter into an agreement, and that if the facts turn out to be incorrect, it will be compensated for the loss it has suffered due to its reliance upon them. Under Turkish law, the intended effect can be achieved by (i) an explicit statement in the SPA that the promising party acknowledges and accepts the other party's reliance on such representations and warranties when signing the agreement, and (ii) an explicit obligation to put the recipient of the representation in the same position as that in which the recipient of the representation or warranty would have been if the representation or warranty was true, accurate and not misleading.

[123] The scope of the representations and warranties of the sellers are shaped by, and varies depending on, the findings of the due diligence. However, it is customary in the share deals in Turkey to include representations and warranties with respect to the authority of the sellers, corporate and capital structure of the target, title and legal status of shares, licenses and authorizations of the target, accounts and financial records, litigation, environmental, regulatory and employment related liabilities, assets, real property, insurance, taxation issues and solvency of the target.

[124] Since a share transfer is considered a sale of shares exclusively under Turkish law, the representations and warranties of the seller must be drafted as fundamental obligations of the seller. In addition, certain representations and warranties are often drafted as independent guarantees of the seller.

9 TAKEOVERS, MANDATORY BIDS

[125] The principles and guidelines governing mandatory and voluntary tender offers applicable to shareholdings in publicly held companies are set out in the CMB's Tender Offer Communiqué No. II-26.1 ('*Tender Offer Communiqué*').

9.1 Mandatory Tender Offer

[126] The shareholders of public companies may either voluntarily offer to purchase the shares of the minority shareholders or under certain circumstances, they are obliged to launch a mandatory tender offer (MTO) to purchase the same. Since the acquisition of shares of public companies may trigger the MTO requirement, this should be taken into account before investing in a public company.

[127] The procedures and principles regarding the execution of an MTO are set out under the Tender Offer Communiqué, through which the tender offer rules in Turkey have been amended and the previous Communiqué No. IV-44 was repealed.

[128] There are a limited number of exceptional MTO cases where the Tender Offer Communiqué does not apply.

9.2 General Principles

[129] Persons who acquire shares or voting rights in a public company through a voluntary tender offeror through block or individual acquisitions which grants them direct or indirect management control, solely or in concert with other persons, are obliged to make an MTO to purchase the shares of the remaining shareholders unless the acquisition triggering the requirement falls under one of the exceptions or the exemptions.

[130] In addition, any change in management control resulting from the execution of special written agreements between the existing shareholders, despite the absence of any change in the ownership of the shares, can also trigger the MTO requirement.

[131] Directly or indirectly holding more than 50% of the voting rights of a public company, solely or in concert with others, or regardless of the percentage of shares, holding privileged shares granting the right to elect the absolute majority of the members of the board of directors or the right to nominate the same number of members in the general assembly is deemed to constitute management control.

[132] It is compulsory to make an application to the CMB within six business days of the acquisition of shares conferring management control, with an information form and other required documentation. The MTO process must be initiated within two months following the occurrence of the event triggering the MTO and within six business days following the approval of the information form by the CMB. The CMB may grant additional time to launch the MTO, provided that interest at an annual rate of Turkish Lira Interbank Offer Rate (TRLIBOR) plus 50% is added to the MTO price for each day following the end of two months where the price is denominated in Turkish Liras. Where the price is determined in EUR or USD, the applicable interest rate is based on Euro Interbank Offered Rate (EURIBOR) or London Interbank Offer Rate (LIBOR) plus 50% respectively. In the event of non-completion of the MTO transaction by the end of the additional time granted by the CMB, an administrative fine up to the amount of the total value of the shares subject to the MTO may be imposed on the persons who have failed to launch such MTO.

[133] The MTO must remain open for a minimum of ten and a maximum of twenty business days. In addition, failure to complete the MTO in the prescribed

periods may result in automatic suspension of the voting rights of the defaulting shareholder and any parties acting in concert, without the need for the CMB's further action. Similarly, such shares are disregarded in determining the general assembly quorum.

9.3 MTO Price

[134] In principle, the payments should be made in full and in cash. However, the MTO price may be paid partially or wholly in listed securities on condition that the written approval of the shareholders is obtained. CMB may request a guarantee for payment of the MTO price by a Turkish bank or a third-party legal entity.

[135] There are different calculation methods for the MTO price depending on whether the public company is listed, whether there is an indirect change of control in the public company, and whether the public company has more than one class of shares.

[136] The MTO price cannot be less than:

(a) if the public company is listed:
   (i) the arithmetic average of the adjusted daily weighted average stock prices that originate in the six-month-period prior to the public disclosure of the management control; or
   (ii) the highest amount paid by the offeror or parties in concert for the same group shares of the public company in the six-month period prior to the MTO trigger date.

(b) if the public company is not listed:
   (i) the price determined in the valuation report prepared in accordance with relevant legislation; or
   (ii) the highest amount paid by the offeror or parties in concert for the same group shares of the public company in the six-month period prior to the MTO trigger date.

[137] Secondary obligations or premiums and similar considerations are also considered for the determination of the MTO price. The CMB may ask a valuation report as of the share transfer date if deemed necessary.

[138] The MTO price is subject to redetermination in the event that the shares of the public company are purchased by the offeror or persons acting in concert with the offeror at a price higher than the MTO price between the date of the public disclosure of the SPA and the expiry date of the MTO. Any redetermined price cannot be lower than the highest price paid for the shares so acquired.

9.4 Exemptions from the MTO Requirement

[139] The MTO requirement would not apply in the circumstances listed in detail under the Tender Offer Communiqué. Below are a few examples of such circumstances:

(1) acquisition of management control subsequent to a voluntary tender offer made to all shareholders for all of the shares under their possession;
(2) acquisition of management control through an approval by the general assembly of special written agreements executed between the existing shareholders and granting of exit rights to participating shareholders whose dissents have been annotated in the general assembly minutes;
(3) without losing the management control, reacquisition of more than 50% of the voting rights of the company by the same shareholder having management control after his shareholding falls below such threshold;
(4) acquisition of management control through share transfers within the same group holding a controlling interest in the public company;
(5) as a result of partial acquisition of shares of shareholders having management control, sharing of the management control equally (or at a lower ratio) with the shareholders having management control before the share transfer by a written contract, provided that the buyer has 50% or less of the voting rights;
(6) Triggering of the right to squeeze out and sell out upon the share acquisition.

[140] In the occurrence of one of the circumstances where an MTO is not triggered, the shareholders who obtain management control must make a public disclosure of such circumstance by indicating the reason why a mandatory tender is not triggered within at least two business days from the date management control is obtained. The CMB may also grant an exemption from the MTO requirement under the circumstances listed in Tender Offer Communiqué upon request. Below are a few examples of such circumstances:

(1) acquisition of the shares further to an obligatory shareholding structure change in order to strengthen the financial position of the company that is in financial distress;
(2) disposal (or an undertaking to make a disposal within a period specified by CMB) of the part of the shares which necessitates the MTO requirement;
(3) change of management control in the parent company of a public company, without aiming to gain control of the public company;
(4) sale of the public shares of a public company under privatization;
(5) change in management control due to a merger transaction provided that the shares of the shareholders who voted against the merger in the related general assembly are acquired;
(6) acquisition of the shares as a result of the bank's enforcement of a security due to the borrower's failure to repay a loan;
(7) acquisition of shares is mandatory pursuant to a legal requirement;
(8) change of management control of the public company as a result of inheritance or the allocation of matrimonial property or other legal obligations.

[141] In order to request an exemption, shareholders who are obliged to make a tender offer must make an application to the CMB within six business days as of the

MTO triggering event. If rejected, the MTO should be initiated within one month as of the date of the CMB decision.

9.5 Voluntary Tender Offers

[142] Any investor (whether or not already a shareholder of the target public company) may launch a tender offer to acquire all or a specified number of shares in a public company. The offeror must apply to the CMB in order to obtain the approval for the voluntary tender offer together with the information and documents set forth in the Tender Offer Communiqué. The duration of the tender offer shall be ten to twenty business days. The actual tender offer process shall be initiated within six business days as of the approval of the tender offer form by the CMB.

[143] The offeror may increase the offer price up until one business day prior to the end of the tender offer process and/or change the price for the other, larger portion or all of the shares, if the initial offer was made for a part of the shares. The new offer must be notified to the CMB and disclosed to the public in order to be valid.

[144] The offeror must make public disclosure of certain matters. These matters are listed in detail under the Tender Offer Communiqué; below are a few examples:

(1) The decision to make a voluntary tender offer.
(2). The triggering of the obligation to make an MTO, whether an exemption will be requested for the MTO, and if so, an explanation for the basis of the exemption.
(3) The price for the tender offer or the information on how the price will be determined.
(4) The result of the application to make a tender offer or the application for an exemption.

[145] At the end of the tender offer process, the total number of shares, share groups and nominal value of shares acquired during the tender offer process and the total number of shareholders who agreed to sell their shares

9.6 Squeeze-Out and sell-Out Options

[146] The CML allows the majority shareholder(s) exceeding a certain shareholding percentage to squeeze-out the minority shareholders and the simultaneous triggering of minority shareholders' right of sell-out to the majority shareholders, the details of which are regulated under the Communiqué No. II-27.3 on Squeeze-out and Sell-out Rights ('*Squeeze-out Communiqué*').

9.6.1 Squeeze-Out

[147] Pursuant to the Squeeze-out Communiqué, the controlling shareholder holding 98% of the total voting rights of a publicly held company is entitled to squeeze-out the minority shareholders,[1] provided that it reaches the 98% following a tender offer or by any other means including acting in concert with others ('*Controlling Shareholder*'). The direct and indirect shares without taking into account the privileges over the shares held by majority shareholders and persons acting in concert, if any, shall be considered for calculation of the 98% ownership of the voting rights. However, additional shares acquired by existing shareholders during unpaid capital increases and/or paid capital increases where the preemption right is not limited or due to inheritance, reacquired shares, suspension of voting rights will not trigger squeeze-out/sell-out rights.

[148] Upon becoming a Controlling Shareholder, application to the publicly held company must be made within two months, failing which the right to squeeze out will lapse. Such application must, *inter alia*, include a letter of guarantee from bank evidence of a deposit to blocked account of the funds that will be used for payment of the purchase price, the calculation of which differs depending on whether the shares in question are listed.

The Calculation of the Purchase Price

[149] The below criteria are considered when determining the price of the squeeze-out and sell-out rights.

(a) For listed shares in the Borsa Istanbul (BIST) Star Market:

> The purchase price is the average of (i) daily weighted average of the stock prices within the last thirty days prior to the disclosure announcing that squeeze-out and sell-out rights have been triggered; and (ii) price for each share group determined under the valuation report.

(b) For listed shares in other markets:

> The purchase price is the average of (i) daily adjusted weighted average of the stock prices determined within the last six months prior to the disclosure announcing that squeeze-out and sell-out rights have been triggered; and (ii) price for each share group determined under the valuation report.

[1] Shareholder(s) of a joint-stock company representing at least 10% of the share capital (5% for publicly held joint-stock company) is deemed as 'minority' and enjoy a certain degree of protection under the TCC and CML. For the purposes of this section, we use 'minority' for the rest of the shareholders rather than representing at least 2% of the share capital of the publicly held joint-stock company.

(c) For non-listed shares:

The price is the squeeze-out and sell-out price set forth in the valuation report which must be attached to the application.

[150] However, if becoming a Controlling Shareholder resulting change in the management control, an MTO price ('MTO price') will also be calculated for both listed companies and non-listed public companies. If the MTO price is higher than the calculated price above, squeeze-out/sell-out price will be the MTO price.

[151] Following the receipt of the squeeze-out application by the publicly held company, the process is as follows:

(i) the company checks that the Controlling Shareholder reached or exceeded the 98% threshold;
(ii) the company evaluates/confirms the purchase price;
(iii) the board of directors adopts a resolution on cancellation of the shares of the minority shareholders and issuance of new shares to the Controlling Shareholder in a number corresponding to the cancelled shares within five business days;
(iv) the company applies to the CMB for the approval of the issuance certificate in relation to the newly issued shares within ten business days of the resolution date; and
(v) application is made to the Istanbul Stock Exchange for delisting in case of a publicly listed company.

9.6.2 Sell-Out

[152] Pursuant to the Squeeze-out Communiqué, following a triggering event for the squeeze-out right of a Controlling Shareholder, the minority shareholders have a right to put their shares to the Controlling Shareholder within the same two-month period as for the squeeze-out right. The two-month period is not suspended even if the holdings of the Controlling Shareholder fall below 98% within such period. The company will carry out a process similar to the process referred to in section 9.6.1. The principles for determination of the squeeze-out right apply *mutatis mutandis* to the sell-out price.

[153] Following the complete exercise of the squeeze-out right or sell-out right and the concentration of all shares in the hands of the Controlling Shareholder, a publicly held company will be deregistered by the CMB.

[154] The price for squeeze-out or sell-out pursuant to the Squeeze-out Communiqué must be paid in full in Turkish Lira.

10 COMMON FINANCING METHODS

10.1 Acquisition Loans

[155] In Turkey, the typical debt funding of acquisition transactions is provided by way of bank loans. Banks usually prefer senior secured debt. The bank providing acquisition financing will scrutinize the project and the associated business plan to determine the amount of the loan and security requirements.

10.1.1 Syndication

[156] In Turkey, syndication usually takes place before the disbursement of a loan since this is significantly more advantageous for stamp tax purposes. The key issue here is that lenders are obliged to pay stamp tax on each syndication after the drawdown. Common practice among Turkish banks is to shift these costs to the borrower, however, this is usually resisted. As a result, post-drawdown syndication is unusual.

10.1.2 Prohibition of Financial Assistance

[157] Since the new TCC came into force in 2012, joint-stock companies are no longer allowed to provide loans or guarantees or grant security on their assets (such as share pledge, mortgage or account pledge) for the purpose of acquisition of their own shares by a third party. Transactions breaching this prohibition are null and void. In order to provide a security structure in light of this new restriction, in practice, the shares of the acquiring entity and the target are pledged to secure the acquisition loan, the acquiring entity and the target are merged as soon as possible and further security is established on the assets of the merged entity.

10.1.3 Tax Treatment of Interest

[158] Interest on loans payable to foreign states, international institutions, foreign banks and foreign corporations which qualify as financial institutions in their country of residence and which provide loans to the public is subject to 0% withholding tax.

10.2 Common Forms of Security

[159] Security under Turkish law can be established in different forms, each having its own defining characteristics but all having the same underlying purpose, namely to confer on the right holder a priority right over the relevant assets when compared to other creditors. The principal security interests are as follows.

10.2.1 Pledge of Shares

[160] In order to perfect the establishment of security over shares of a joint-stock company that are in physical form, the shares to be pledged should be endorsed with a pledge endorsement (blank endorsement) and the shares should be physically delivered by the pledgor to the pledgee. Following the completion of the delivery and endorsement, a board resolution in relation to the registration of the pledge into the share ledger of the company should be adopted and the registration of the same should be completed. If the shares of the company are dematerialized and registered, the pledge can be created by notifying such pledge to the relevant custody authority (*Merkezi Kayıt Kuruluşu*), in the records of such authority, instead of having endorsed and delivered the physical possession. All other steps remain the same.

10.2.2 Pledge of Bank Accounts

[161] The establishment of a pledge over a bank account is possible through a written pledge agreement. In order to make such pledge practically effective for the pledgee, the pledge should be notified to the relevant account bank. Obtaining the acknowledgement of the account bank to the creation of the pledge (to be sure whether there is another privileged right or claim of a third party or the account bank, over such pledged account) is the common market practice even if it is not a legal requirement.

10.2.3 Assignment of Receivables

[162] A pledge cannot be established on an agreement but on the receivables arising out of the agreement. In order to establish such a pledge, receivables from such agreements are assigned to the creditor with the purpose of creating security through a written agreement. The consent of the debtor of the assigned receivables is not required but the debtor must be notified of the assignment of receivables.

10.2.4 Movable Pledge in Commercial Transactions

[163] The Law on Movable Pledge in Commercial Transactions ('Movable Pledge Law') entered into force as of 1 January 2017 and replaced the concept of the commercial enterprise pledge under Turkish law. Law No. 6750 institutes a central pledge registry ('Pledge Registry') which enables creation of a pledge over moveable assets by registration therewith without the delivery of physical possession of the moveable asset.

[164] Law No. 6750 allows a pledge to be established over receivables, intellectual property and industrial rights, raw materials, animals, licenses, rental proceeds, tenancy rights, moveable operating equipment, stock and machinery, consumable goods, stocks and instruments, agricultural products, commercial title and/or trade name, commercial enterprises and commercial trade names. Moreover, future moveable assets and existing or future proceeds of commercial enterprises may be pledged.

[165] Law No. 6750 also allows the pledgee to demand transfer of ownership of the pledged asset if the pledge is a first-ranking security.

[166] Both banks and financial institutions as well as any commercial business (provided that the pledge agreement is executed between merchants/craftsmen) may act as pledgee under the Movable Pledge Law although banks and financial institutions will benefit from certain tax exemptions in establishing the pledge.

10.2.5 Mortgages

[167] In order to duly establish a mortgage on real property, an official mortgage deed must be prepared ex officio by the title deed registry where the property is located and such mortgage must be registered with the same registry. If the mortgage will be established in foreign currency, the receivables which the mortgage secures and the limit of the amount secured by the mortgage should be in the same currency.

10.3 Stamp Tax

[168] For an overview, please refer to section 16 below.

11 TRANSFORMATIONS

11.1 General Framework

[169] The general framework for corporate transformations is set out in the TCC. Its provisions on mergers and demergers, which are largely based on Directive 78/855/EEC and Directive 82/891/EEC concerning mergers and demergers, respectively, and the Swiss Federal Act on Merger, Demerger, Conversion and Transfer of Assets and Liabilities (*Bundesgesetz über die Fusion, Spaltung, Umwandlung und Vermögensübertragung*), provide for a comprehensive regulation of mergers, demergers and conversions of legal entities.

[170] In terms of scope, the rules governing corporate transformations under the TCC are applicable to all types of commercial companies, i.e., cooperatives, general partnerships, limited partnerships, joint-stock companies and limited liability companies, as well as to sole proprietorships registered in the Commercial Register.

11.2 Mergers

[171] The TCC differentiates between two types of mergers: acquisition and combination, and the legal provisions governing both types of mergers are similar to a large extent.

11.2.1 Merger by Acquisition

[172] In the event of a merger by acquisition, one or more companies are dissolved without liquidation, struck off the Commercial Register and their business assets, including all rights and obligations, are transferred to the surviving company involved in the merger (the acquiring company) by operation of law. In principle, shareholders of the transferor (dissolving) companies become shareholders in the acquiring company: the acquiring company increases its share capital to the extent such increase is necessary to preserve the rights of members of the transferring company. Their shareholding in the successor company is determined by the proportion of the asset value of their shareholdings in the transferor companies to the asset value of the acquiror company.

11.2.2 Merger by Combination

[173] In contrast, in a merger by combination, two or more companies are dissolved without liquidation, struck off the Commercial Register and their business assets, including all rights and obligations, are transferred to a newly established company by operation of law. In principle, the shareholders of the dissolving companies become shareholders in the newly established company. Their shareholding is calculated in accordance with section 11.2.1 above.

11.2.3 Permitted Mergers

[174] The TCC provides an exhaustive list of permitted mergers:

- (i) capital companies and cooperatives may merge:
  - (a) with capital companies and cooperatives; and
  - (b) in an acquiring capacity, with limited and general partnerships.
- (ii) limited and general partnerships may merge:
  - (a) with limited and general partnerships; and
  - (b) in a transferring capacity, with capital companies and cooperatives.

11.2.4 Merger of Companies in Liquidation or with Capital Loss

[175] It is possible to merge a commercial company in liquidation provided that it enters into the merger as the transferring entity and the distribution of its surplus assets upon liquidation has not yet begun. Further, a commercial company which has lost half of its share capital and legal reserves or whose liabilities exceeds its assets, may merge with a commercial company, provided that the latter has freely utilizable equity in at least the amount of the shortfall, and where applicable, in at least the amount of the excess liabilities.

[176] In cases of mergers of commercial companies with a capital loss or whose liabilities exceed its assets or in liquidation, the acquiring company must submit to the Commercial Register evidence that the above-mentioned requirements have been complied with.

11.2.5 Merger Process

(i) The merger process involves the following steps:

(a) Merger agreement: The management bodies of the participating companies enter into a written merger agreement, the relevant content of which is specified by the TCC. The merger agreement must specify, *inter alia*: (a) the share exchange ratio and, if any, compensation payment and equalization payment and details of membership rights of shareholders or partners of transferor company in the transferee; (b) any special advantages granted to management bodies; (c) the date from which the transactions of the transferor shall be treated for accounting purposes as being those of the transferee; and (d) the rights conferred by the transferee on holders of preferential rights/shares without voting rights or profit-sharing certificates.

(b) Interim balance sheet: The merging companies draw up an interim balance sheet, if upon concluding the merger agreement the last balance sheets of the merging companies are more than six months old or if significant changes in the assets and liabilities have occurred.

(c) Merger report: The companies must issue a merger report, explaining and justifying the merger from an economic and legal perspective. In case of a merger by combination, the articles of association of the newly established company shall be attached to the report.

(d) General assembly: The management body shall submit the merger agreement to the general assembly for approval and such approval resolution shall be subject to qualified majority requirements. The qualified majority requirements for capital companies, which account for a considerable portion of the companies in Turkey, are as follows: (a) for joint-stock companies, at least three-quarters majority of the votes represented at the general assembly and the absolute majority of the share capital; and (b) for limited liability companies, at least three-quarters majority of all partners provided that they also represent at least three-quarters of the share capital.

(e) Right of inspection: Before the general assembly resolution, the shareholders or partners of the companies must have at least thirty days to inspect the merger agreement, the merger report, as well as the annual reports for the preceding three business years. These documents shall be deposited at a specified place for inspection by the shareholders or partners. Provided that all shareholders' or partners' consent is obtained, small and medium-sized enterprises may dispense with the right of inspection.

(f) Registration of the merger: Following the adoption of general assembly resolutions, registration of the merger is made before the Commercial Register, upon which the merger becomes legally effective. All assets and liabilities of the transferring company are transferred to the surviving company by operation of law upon the registration. If the acquiring company is required to increase its share capital following the merger, the amendment to the articles of association regarding the capital increase must be submitted to the Commercial Register as well. Upon the registration of the merger, the transferring company is struck off the Commercial Register.

(ii) Exchange of shares and payments of compensation:

Pursuant to the continuity of membership principle, the shareholders or partners of the transferring company are entitled to participation and rights in the acquiring company equal to their former participation and rights, having regard to the net assets of the merging entities, the allotment of voting rights and as well as other circumstances.

Further, as a reflection of this principle, a supplementary payment in cash – the so-called *equalization payment* – to equalize the share exchange ratio may be provided for in addition to the shares. The equalization payment cannot exceed one-tenth of the newly issued shares.

However, the TCC permits a restriction of the principle of continuity of membership by way of a *compensation payment*. The merging companies may, by way of a provision in the merger agreement:

(a) allow the shareholders or partners to choose either shares in the acquiring company or a compensation payment ('voluntary compensation payment'); or

(b) provide for compensation payment only ('compulsory compensation payment').

The adoption of the merger agreement that provides voluntary compensation payment or compulsory compensation payment requires the agreement of at least 90% of the shareholders or partners with voting rights in the transferring company. The compensation can be paid in cash or in any other form such as shares of another company. Having said that, pursuant to the Merger and Demerger Communiqué No. II-23.2 issued by the CMB, if the merging company is a listed joint-stock company, only publicly traded shares or cash can be provided as compensation to the minority shareholders who are to be squeezed-out. This being the case, the compensation must be paid in cash if such minority shareholder demands it so.

(iii) Simplified merger:

The TCC allows capital companies to merge under a simplified process if:

(a) the acquiring company holds all shares conferring voting rights in the transferring company;

(b) a company or an individual or a group related by law or contract holds all shares conferring voting rights in the merging companies.

In case of a parent-subsidiary merger or a merger of sister companies (i.e., both wholly owned by the same parent), the following requirements do not apply:

(a) merger report;

(b) right of inspection; or

(c) general assembly approval of the merger agreement.

In such cases, the resolution to merge is at the discretion of the management body, unless further decisions that are under the sole authority of the general assembly, such as a capital increase, are required.

Further, if the acquiring company does not hold all, but at least 90% of the shares conferring voting rights in the transferring company, a simplified merger process can also be carried out if:

(a) the minority shareholders are offered with compensation payment (as referred to in section 11.2.5(ii)) being equal to the actual value of the shares as an alternative to the shares in the acquiring company; and

(b) the merger does not result in minority shareholders having to make supplementary payment contributions or result in them providing personal performance or assuming personal liability.

Under these circumstances, merging companies are again not required to draw up a merger report or submit the merger agreement to the general assembly for approval. However, the right of inspection will be granted at least thirty days prior to the application for registration of the merger in the Commercial Register.

11.2.6 Change in the Assets

[177] Due to the merger control rules (*see* section 13 below), a long time can pass between the execution of the merger agreement and approval of the same in the general assembly. If considerable change in the assets or liabilities of one of the merging companies occurs in the interim, its management body is obliged to inform the general assembly and as well as the management bodies of other companies involved in merger.

[178] The management bodies of all legal entities involved in merger then assess whether to amend the merger agreement or relinquish the merger. In the latter case, the management bodies are required to withdraw the submission for general assembly approval, and in the former, they will explain the reasons why the merger agreement is not needed to be amended.

11.2.7 Notice to Creditors

[179] Pursuant to Article 157 of the TCC, the acquiring company is obliged to secure the claims of the creditors of the merging companies, if such creditors request within three months starting from the legally effective date of merger. The merging companies shall inform the creditors of their rights through its website and three notices in the Commercial Register Gazette with seven day intervals between each. The company, instead of providing security, may satisfy any claim to the extent that other creditors are not adversely affected.

11.3 Demerger

[180] Capital companies and cooperatives can be divided into capital companies and cooperatives. These entities may not be divided into partnerships or *vice-versa*.

11.3.1 Types of Demergers

[181] There are different types of demergers under Turkish law. Distinctions may be made as split-up or spin-off and symmetric or asymmetric demerger.

(i) Split-up or Spin-off

[182] In demerger by splitting, where the de-merged entity dissolves without being liquated, the property (assets and liabilities) of the de-merged company is transferred to:

(a) newly established companies; and/or
(b) already existing successor companies.

[183] However, in demerger by spin-off, where the de-merged entity survives the demerger, part of the property (assets and liabilities) of the de-merged company is transferred to:

(a) newly established companies; and/or
(b) already existing successor companies.

[184] Both in split-ups and spin-offs, the shareholders or partners of the de-merged entity receive equity and membership rights in the acquiring legal entity(ies) and the assets subject to spin-off are, as is in mergers, are transferred on the basis of general subrogation, regardless of the underlying transaction type, and no transfer of the respective assets as capital in kind occurs.

(ii) Symmetric or Asymmetric Demerger

[185] The continuity of membership principle in the merger applies *mutatis mutandis*. Accordingly, the shareholders or partners of the de-merged company are entitled to participation and rights in the acquiring company equal to their former participation and rights.

[186] In a symmetric demerger, the shareholders or partners of the de-merged company are to be granted with equity and membership rights in all companies involved in the demerger, proportional to their former shares. For instance, company E owned equally by A, B, C and D spins off and transfers its property to company X, which is equally owned by Y and Z. If the symmetric demerger is chosen, A, B, C and D will each receive 25% of the newly issued shares of company X.

[187] By contrast, in an asymmetric demerger, the shareholders or partners of the de-merged company are to be granted equity and membership rights in certain or all of the companies involved in the demerger, changing their proportional ownership interests, which in particular could be preferred for dissolving joint-ventures or management buy-outs. For instance, A, B and C holds 40%, 30% and 30%, respectively, of the shares of company X. Following the asymmetric spin-off, A and B may be the only shareholders of the newly established company Z, and C may hold the majority of the shares of the company X, where it held only 30% prior to the demerger. Whilst an asymmetric demerger is likely to breach the continuity of membership principle, at least 90% of the shareholders or partners with voting rights in the transferring (de-merged) company must approve such demerger.

[188] Equalization payments not exceeding 10% of the actual value of the shares issued are allowed in demergers as well, however, contrary to mergers, the TCC does not provide compensation payment in demergers. There is no prevailing opinion on this aspect. While it is suggested that in consideration of the flexibility of the asymmetric demerger, a squeeze-out of minority shareholders may be possible in the asymmetric demerger as well, it is also argued that TCC specifically does not allow compensation payments in demergers by neither providing an express provision nor referring to applicability of the relevant provision on the mergers to demergers.

11.3.2 Formalities

[189] The demerger process is similar to the merger process. The most important steps are the following.

Demerger Agreement/Demerger Plan

[190] The management bodies of participating companies shall enter into a written demerger agreement, the relevant content of which is specified by the TCC. If, however, a company will transfer its property via demerger to newly established companies, it shall prepare a demerger plan. The contract/plan shall, *inter alia*, set out: (a) the terms related to share exchange and, if any, the amount of equalization payment and explanations in relation to the rights of members of the transferor company in the transferee; (b) a list of employment relationships to be transferred with the demerger; (c) special advantages granted to management bodies; (d) the date from which the transactions of the transferor shall be treated for accounting purposes as being those of the transferee; and (e) an inventory containing a clear description and allocation of the property, business parts, real property. What happens with unallocated assets depends on the type of demerger: In case an asset (including intangible assets or receivables as well) has not been allocated by the demerger agreement/plan, it shall be jointly owned by the transferees proportionally to the net assets which will be transferred as per the demerger agreement/plan or continue to belong to the spin-off company, in split-up and in spin-off, respectively.

Interim Balance Sheet

[191] The commercial companies involved in the demerger shall draw up an interim balance sheet, if upon concluding the demerger agreement/plan, the date of last balance sheet is more than six months old, or if material changes regarding the assets and liabilities have occurred.

Demerger Report

[192] The companies must issue a demerger report, explaining and justifying the demerger from an economic and legal perspective. In case the transferee will be a newly established company, the articles of association of the newly established company shall be attached to the report. The report shall set out, *inter alia*, specific details of share valuation; effects of the demerger on employees and creditors of the companies involved in the demerger.

General Assembly

[193] The management body shall submit the demerger agreement/plan to the general assembly for approval and such approval resolution shall be subject to qualified majority requirements. The qualified majority requirements in merger process apply *mutatis mutandis*.

Right of Inspection

[194] Before the general assembly resolution, the shareholders or partners of the companies must have at least two months to inspect the demerger agreement/plan, the demerger report, as well as the annual reports for the preceding three business years. These documents shall be deposited in a particular place for the inspection of the shareholders or partners. Provided that all shareholders' or partners' consent is obtained, small and medium-sized enterprises may dispense with the right of inspection.

Registration of the Merger

[195] Following the adoption of general assembly resolutions, registration of the demerger in the Commercial Register, upon which the merger becomes legally effective, may be applied for. All assets and liabilities of the transferring company are transferred by operation of law through the registration. If the transferor company is required to decrease its share capital following the demerger, the amendment in the articles of association regarding the capital decrease shall be submitted to the Commercial Register as well. Upon the registration of the split-up, the transferring company shall be struck off the Commercial Register.

11.3.3 Creditors' Protection

[196] As opposed to mergers, demergers deprive the transferor's creditors of assets, which results in entitling creditors with more protection in comparison to a merger.

(i) Pre-transaction Notice to Creditors

[197] The creditors of the legal entities in a demerger shall be notified, as opposed to mergers, *prior* to the demerger by publication three times in Turkish Commercial Register Gazette with seven days intervals between each and via web-page to make their claims and demand security for the same. It is an obligation for the companies involved in demerger to secure the creditors if latter so demands within three months following the notification. Such obligation may be waived if it can be proved that the demerger will not compromise the claims of the creditors.

[198] As in merger, the company, instead of providing security, may satisfy any claim to the extent that other creditors are not adversely affected.

(ii) Secondary Liability of the Companies

[199] Other companies involved in the demerger, being secondarily liable, shall be jointly and severally liable for the claims that have not been paid by the primarily liable company, the company to which such claims were assigned through the merger agreement/plan.

[200] This would become more of an issue if any of the companies is subject to further investment. Consequently, it would be wise to carry out the relevant due diligence for the *other companies* if, for e.g., a share purchase at a company that was previously involved in a demerger is intended.

[201] Secondarily liable companies may be prosecuted, provided that the claim has not been secured and primarily liable company:

(a) is bankrupt;
(b) has obtained a period for concordat;
(c) has been sued for debt enforcement until a final certificate is issued;
(d) has relocated its registered address abroad and, therefore, may no longer be prosecuted in Turkey; and
(e) has changed its registered address abroad, and therefore, to pursue the enforcement of the debt is seriously affected.

11.4 Transformation of a Legal Form

[202] It is possible to transform a company's legal form to another without liquidation. The company with the new legal form remains the same legal entity as prior to the transformation, i.e., it is not dissolved. The transformation of the legal form of a company requires registration in the Commercial Register. The permitted legal form to which a company may be transformed into depend on the type of company being transformed.

11.4.1 Permitted Transformations

[203] The TCC provides an exhaustive list of permitted transformations:

(i) A capital company may transform into:
  (a) a capital company in another form; and
  (b) a cooperative.
(ii) a general partnerships may transform into:
  (a) a capital company;
  (b) a cooperative; and
  (c) a limited partnership.
(iii) a limited partnership may transform into:
  (a) a capital company;
  (b) a cooperative; and
  (c) a general partnership.
(iv) a cooperative may transform into a capital company.

11.4.2 Equity and Membership Rights

[204] Pursuant to the continuity of membership principle, the equity and membership rights of members shall be preserved in transformations as well. This being the case, in the exchange for preferential rights or profit-sharing certificates, either equivalent rights shall be granted or, an appropriate compensation for preferential rights and actual value of the profit-sharing certificates shall be paid.

11.4.3 Transformation process

[205] Interim balance sheet, transformation plan, transformation report, right of inspection, general assembly approval and registration of transformation in merger and de-merger processes apply *mutatis mutandis* in the case of transformations.

[206] The management body shall submit the transformation plan to the general assembly for approval and such approval resolution shall be subject to qualified majority requirements. The qualified majority requirements for capital companies are as follows:

(i) for joint-stock companies and partnerships limited by shares, at least two-thirds majority of the votes represented at the general assembly and at least two-thirds majority of the share capital represented, and if supplementary capital contributions or other obligations to provide specific performance are resolved in the transformation into a limited liability company, the approval of all shareholders is required;

(ii) for the transformation of a capital company into a cooperative, the approval of all shareholders; and for limited liability companies, at least three-quarters majority of members who at the same time hold three-quarters of the share capital.

12 LABOUR LAW AND EMPLOYMENT CONSIDERATIONS

12.1 General Introduction

[207] Employment in Turkey is mainly regulated by the Labour Law, the Social Security Law No. 5510 ('*Social Security Law*') and also various laws and regulations on specific issues in Labour Law.

12.2 Employment Contracts

[208] Labour Law defines an employment contract as 'a contract consisting of two undertakings; the employee undertakes to work dependently and the employer undertakes to make the relevant payments in return'. The relationship arising from this contract is called an employment relationship established between the employee and the employer. Even though the relationship comes into existence upon the execution of the employment contract, certain other rights arise at times set by the legislation such as paid annual leave and severance payments. Precedent establishes that the most important aspect of the employment relationship can be observed when the contract is claimed to be null and void; due to the employment relationship the contract will be treated as valid.

[209] In principle, there is no obligation to obtain employees' consent for a share or asset sale under employment legislation in Turkey. Having said that, employees can object to their employment contracts being transferred to the buyer if such transfer results from a merger or demerger. According to the TCC, in the event of a merger or demerger, the employment contracts are also transferred to the buyer with all its right and obligations, provided that the employee does not object to this transfer. The employees are entitled to object on an individual basis to the transfer of their employment contract. Where an objection is made by the employee, the employee's employment will terminate at the end of the legal notice period. In such circumstances, the employee will be entitled to full severance payment from the buyer.

[210] The Labour Law provides that if a business is transferred in whole or in part to a new employer, the employment contracts which are in force must be transferred to the new employer together with all associated rights and liabilities.

[211] When employment contracts are transferred to a new employer, the employees are entitled to terminate the employment contract on the basis of just cause.

Further, an adjustment is usually made to the employment conditions of the sellers' employees and the buyer's existing employees. If the employment conditions of the sellers' employees become less favourable than before, they are entitled to terminate the employment contract on the basis of just cause. In these circumstances, the employees are entitled to a severance payment. The seller and buyer are jointly liable for making the severance payment to the employee.

[212] The severance compensation entitlement is thirty days' salary for each year of service to the company. There is a ceiling for the maximum amount of monthly salary to be taken into consideration for the calculation. For the second half of 2020, this ceiling was set at TL7 117.17.

[213] Employment contracts are not affected by a share sale. Since employment contracts are executed between the employee and the target company as the employer, a change in the employer's shareholding structure does not affect the employee. In this case, neither the employer nor the employees are entitled to terminate the contract due to such change.

[214] If the new employer, i.e., the buyer, wishes to terminate the employment contract, the employee has the right to claim notice and severance payments. In addition, the employee may file a reemployment lawsuit against the buyer.

[215] If there is a collective bargaining agreement, the provisions of such agreement should be taken into account during the determination of the obligations of the transferor and transferee parties against the employee.

[216] In addition, the employee and the employer can agree on a non-compete clause which will be effective after the termination of the employment contract for a period of up to two years.

[217] Under Turkish law, there is no employees' committee or similar organization established in companies as a management body. Accordingly, the employees do not play an active role in the decision-making process.

13 MERGER CONTROL

[218] The main source of competition law in Turkey is the Act on Protection of Competition, No. 4054 and the TCA is the competent authority. The main secondary legislation regarding merger clearance is the Communiqué No. 2010/4 on Mergers and Acquisitions Subject to the Approval of the Turkish Competition Board ('*Merger Communiqué*'). EU competition law and European Merger Control are not applicable in Turkey but the TCA does tend to follow a similar approach to that adopted by the European Commission in many instances.

13.1 Scope of Controls and Timetable

13.1.1 Notification Requirement

[219] A merger or acquisition transaction must be notified to the Competition Board for approval if:

(i) the proposed transaction results in a permanent change of control in the Target; and
(ii) the prescribed turnover thresholds are met (*see* section 13.1.5 below).

13.1.2 Filing

[220] The notification must be filed together with copies of the documentation containing the main terms and conditions of the transaction. There is no specific deadline for making a filing but the merger notification must be filed and the clearance must be obtained prior to closing. It is possible to make a notification with a draft agreement, a term sheet or a memorandum of understanding prior to its finalization, which reduces the risk that the notification procedure will delay the completion of the transaction.

13.1.3 Assessment

[221] Upon receipt of the notification, the TCA makes an assessment as to whether the transaction would result in creating or strengthening a dominant position in the relevant market. For straightforward transactions, the assessment takes about four to six weeks if the application contains all of the required information and documentation. Additional information and documents may be requested by the case handlers during the course of their evaluation. After completing its review, the TCA may either approve the transaction or decide to initiate a final examination process (a Phase 2 investigation). A Phase 2 investigation takes about six months and this period may be extended once for an additional period of up to six months by the TCA if it deems this to be necessary.

13.1.4 Information Required for the Turkish Competition Law Notification Analysis

[222] In order to evaluate whether any transaction will result in a permanent change of control, the before/after completion control structure needs to be evaluated. In this respect, information on the before/after completion shareholding structure and the decision-making quorums, as well as any arrangements between the shareholders, such as the scope of veto rights, if any, should be analysed.

13.1.5 Notification Thresholds

[223] According to the Merger Communiqué, a transaction must be notified to the TCA if the parties satisfy one of the following turnover tests:

(i) the aggregate annual turnover of the parties generated in Turkey exceeds TL750 m (*approx. EUR71.9 m*); *and*
(ii) at least two of the parties each have an annual turnover of TL250 m (*approx. EUR23.9 m*) or more generated in Turkey; *or*
(iii) the total worldwide annual turnover of one of the parties exceeds TL3 bn (*approx. EUR287.8 m*); *and*
(iv) the annual turnover of at least one of the other parties generated in Turkey exceeds TL250 m (*approx. EUR23.9 m*).

[224] However, according to the recent amendments introduced to the Merger Communique in 2022, technology undertakings are exempted from the local turnover thresholds given in (ii) and (iv) above. This exemption applies to any technology undertaking that (i) is active in the Turkish geographical market, (ii) conducts R&D activities in the Turkish geographical market or (iii) provides services to users in Turkey. Accordingly, in order to catch 'killer acquisitions' most of the transactions concerning technology undertakings will require filing in Turkey, even if the target company has no turnover. Under the Merger Communiqué, technology undertakings are defined as undertakings or assets operating in the field of (i) digital platforms, (ii) software (including gaming), (iii) financial technologies, (iv) biotechnology, (v) pharmacology, (vi) agrochemicals, and (vii) health technologies. That said, since the Merger Communique provides a broad definition of technology undertakings, notifiability analysis shall be made case-by-case basis.

[225] For this purpose, turnover is the net sales figures generated during the financial year preceding the date of the notification or, if this cannot be calculated, of those generated during the financial year ending closest to the date of the notification. Intra-group sales are not taken into account in the turnover calculations.

13.2 Failure to Notify the TCA

[226] According to the relevant Turkish legislation, any transaction which is completed without the required notification filing may be declared null and void until the competition clearance is obtained. If the TCA discovers that a transaction has been completed without a notification, the TCA will ex officio require the parties to file a notification for the transaction. Then, as a result of its examination:

(i) the TCA may approve the transaction and impose an administrative fine on the acquiring party equal to 0.1% of its gross turnover generated in the previous financial year; and
(ii) if the TCA finds that the transaction raises competition concerns, in addition to imposing the above fine, it may decide to order the cancellation of

the transaction and the reversal of all arrangements resulting from the transaction;

(iii) if a transaction leads to the creation or strengthening of a dominant position in the market, then more significant monetary fines may be imposed and such transaction may be deemed invalid;

(iv) the TCA may also impose fines on the executive members or employees of the undertakings who have played a significant role in the failure to file or complete the transaction without the approval of the TCA. This fine may be up to 5% of the fine imposed on the undertakings.

[227] The legislation does not make a clear distinction regarding the basis of the calculation of monetary fines. It has a discretion to take either the world-wide or the Turkish turnover as a basis for the calculation of the fine. According to previous experience, the turnover figure generated in the Republic of Turkey is usually taken into account.

13.3 Ancillary Restraints

[228] Ancillary restraints such as non-compete and non-solicitation obligations are frequently used in mergers and acquisitions transactions in Turkey. As a rule of thumb, a period of three years is considered acceptable for ancillary restraint by the TCA. In addition, such restrictions shall be objective and directly related to the transaction, and geographic area should be reasonable.

13.4 Remedial Measures and Conditional Clearance

[229] It is very uncommon for TCA to block transactions upon merger clearance applications. TCA may, however, give conditional clearances. According to the current practice of the TCA, conditions are based on remedies suggested by the parties. Conditions may be structural or behavioural. The main aim of such conditions is to maintain the structure of competition in the market before the transaction. Consequently, solutions that create a structural change in the market, especially like the disposal of a specific unit of business, which (i) yield sustainable and short-term results to eliminate competition issues and (ii) do not require supervision after application, are more preferred by the TCA.

13.5 Other Turkish Competition Rules Affecting Competitive Behaviour

[230] Dominant position is described as the power to act and determine economic parameters independently from customers and competitors. Being in a dominant position is not per se prohibited under Turkish competition law. Abuse of dominant position is prohibited and such abuse is possible either by an individual or collective acts or through agreements.

[231] Anti-competitive agreements and concerted practices are prohibited under the Turkish competition law which includes direct or indirect restriction of competition via vertical and/or horizontal agreements or practices. There are group exemptions for vertical agreements and specific sectors as well as for research and development and technology transfer activities and obtaining individual exemptions is possible.

14 INSOLVENCY PROCEEDINGS

[232] Insolvency proceedings in Turkish law are governed by the TCC and the Enforcement and Bankruptcy Law No. 2004 (‘*Enforcement and Bankruptcy Law*’). Under Turkish law, as a rule, only ‘*merchants*’ can be the subject of bankruptcy. A ‘merchant’ is defined in Article 11 of the TCC as: ‘a natural person who manages a commercial enterprise on his/her own behalf’. In addition, the TCC provides that collective companies, commandite companies, joint-stock companies, limited liability companies and cooperatives are deemed as merchants, and are therefore subject to the bankruptcy regime.

[233] Under Turkish law, insolvency occurs when a company is unable to meet its liabilities as they come due to its current assets. If a company is insolvent, bankruptcy may be declared on the basis of a petition filed by the debtor or a petition filed by one or more creditors. The commercial court decides whether the company is bankrupt.

[234] A creditor may start enforcement proceedings by applying to the enforcement office for unpaid debts of legal or natural persons who are subject to the bankruptcy regime. After having served the payment order from the enforcement office, the creditor may file a petition to the commercial court to request the declaration of the debtor’s bankruptcy.

[235] In some circumstances, the Enforcement and Bankruptcy Law does not stipulate these steps and it gives a right to apply directly to the commercial court for declaration of debtor’s bankruptcy. These circumstances are specified in detail below.

14.1 Bankruptcy

[236] Any creditor may raise a bankruptcy claim against a debtor who can be subject to the bankruptcy regime at the enforcement office in the district of the debtor (‘*Enforcement Office*’). The creditor may initiate ordinary bankruptcy proceedings for any kind of debt against the debtor without having any bill of exchange (cheques or promissory notes). Debts arising from bills of exchanges can be the subject of special bankruptcy proceedings by application to the Enforcement Office by attaching the bill of exchange to the bankruptcy petition. Upon application of the creditor, the enforcement officer sends a payment order to the debtor. If debtor does not object to the payment order, it will become final and creditor must bring a case before the commercial court for declaration of the debtor's bankruptcy. If the debtor objects to the payment order within the term stipulated for each proceeding, bankruptcy proceeding will cease and the creditor must bring a claim to the commercial court for annulment of objection and declaration of debtor's bankruptcy.

14.1.1 Direct Bankruptcy

[237] In some cases, referred to as 'direct bankruptcy proceedings', a debtor may be declared bankrupt without a payment order. Direct bankruptcy can be demanded by both creditor and the debtor.

[238] A creditor can apply for direct bankruptcy where:

- the debtor does not have a known residence;
- the debtor fails in any way to its commitments;
- the debtor engages or attempts to engage in fraudulent acts breaching the rights of its creditors;
- the debtor conceals its property during the compulsory execution by way of attachment;
- the debtor has suspended its payments;
- a concordat is not approved (for more detail on concordat, *see* section 14.11 below);
- the creditor's claim based on a court decision has not been paid although its payment has been demanded pursuant to an order of execution; or
- the debtor company's debts exceed its current assets.

[239] Direct bankruptcy may also take place at the debtor's request. A debtor can apply to a court to declare itself bankrupt. This can occur in two circumstances:

(i) Technical Bankruptcy:

> When a company suffers losses which reduce its paid up share capital by two-thirds, the board of directors is required to call an extraordinary general assembly meeting. At this meeting, the shareholders must resolve either to compensate the company in cash for the accumulated loss or to decrease the company's paid -up share capital to one-third of its existing share capital
> If the shareholders do not take one of these steps, the board of directors is required to file a lawsuit before the relevant Commercial Court of First Instance to request the court to declare the company bankruptcy lawsuit, each director shall be personally and jointly and severally liable for any and all real damages, incurred by the creditors and the shareholders of such company.

(ii) Obligatory bankruptcy:

The debtor (which is a real person or a general or limited partnership) must apply to a court for bankruptcy if:
- an attachment is ordered against a debtor which results in the debtor losing one-half of its assets; and
- the debtor's remaining assets are insufficient to meet its other debts which will be due and payable within one year.

14.2 Effects of Insolvency Proceedings

[240] By the initiation of bankruptcy proceedings, the court may order protective measures which the court deems necessary for the protection of the creditors. The enforcement office is required to execute the court's orders. In addition, the court may require a written guarantee from the creditor(s) who demand protective measures to secure compensation of the debtor for losses resulting from the protective measures, in case of improper bankruptcy proceedings. If the debtor has not objected to the payment order or claim resulting from the court order, the court will not normally require a guarantee. A creditor who initiates the proceeding is liable for the expenses that may arise until the initial creditors' meeting. Such creditor may also require the issuance of a property register of the debtor's current assets at the time of the initiation of the court proceedings.

14.3 Decision on Bankruptcy

[241] Under Turkish law commercial courts decide whether debtor is insolvent. For ordinary and special insolvency proceedings before the commercial court, the finalized bankruptcy proceeding with the bankruptcy office must be published in wide-circulation newspapers as well as in the Commercial Register Gazette. Within fifteen days from the announcement of bankruptcy petition, other creditors may involve themselves in the case either by filing a claim for dismissal or acceptance of bankruptcy demand. If there is no objection filed, or objections that have been filed are dismissed, the commercial court will decide on depository injunction which grants a right to pay or deposit the debt with accrued interest and expenses to the debtor within seven days from the delivery of depository injunction to the debtor. If debtor pays or deposits such amount to the court, bankruptcy case will be dismissed. If the debtor does not, the debtor will be declared bankrupt by the court with the condition that the creditor who petitioned for the bankruptcy must post security for costs and all notification expenses required for legal remedies of bankruptcy decision until the initial creditors meeting. After the deposit of this amount with the commercial court by the creditor, the court declares the debtor's bankruptcy. This decision can be appealed in ten days.

[242] For direct bankruptcy proceedings, the same procedures apply as for ordinary proceedings, provided that the court may issue a bankruptcy decision without a depository injunction option.

[243] After the notification of bankruptcy decision to bankruptcy office, bankruptcy office must send a notification to the relevant authorities about bankruptcy decision immediately. These authorities can be listed as follows: Title deed registry, Commercial Register, custom administration, postal administration, local chamber of commerce, chamber of industry and stock exchange, local notaries, banks, public administration, tax administration, Ministry of Commerce, Turkish Banks Association, Capital Market Board and other relevant authorities.

14.4 Declaration of Bankruptcy

14.4.1 Effects of Declaration of Bankruptcy on the Debtor's Assets

[244] All attachable assets of debtor are included in the bankruptcy estate (*iflas masası*). These assets can include the debtor's movable and immovable properties, cash, receivables, joint or several title shares, right of usufruct, inheritance share, fiscal rights on intellectual property. Pledged assets of the debtor are included in bankruptcy estate but subject to the pledgee's right of preference.

14.4.2 Effects of Declaration of Bankruptcy to Debtor

[245] The main effect of bankruptcy proceedings on the debtor is that all unpaid debts of the debtor become due by the declaration of bankruptcy.

[246] Insolvency proceedings do not limit the debtor's capacity to act. Debtors have the power of disposition on the assets which are not included in the bankruptcy estate. Although debtor still remains the owner of assets included in bankruptcy estate, it does not have the right to dispose of them. After the declaration of bankruptcy, any disposition by the debtor of bankruptcy estate is null and void.

[247] Since a bankruptcy proceeding is a full proceeding (*külli takip*) and all the creditors are treated equally, there is no need to have separate enforcement proceedings. For that reason, at the bankruptcy proceedings, enforcement claims that have been directed to the debtor stops and no new proceeding can be claimed against the debtor.

[248] Pending lawsuits involving the debtor as plaintiff or defendant, which involve assets included within the bankruptcy estate, are suspended pending the bankruptcy proceedings.

14.5 Liquidation of Assets

[249] After the declaration of debtor's bankruptcy, attachable assets and the receivables of debtor are deemed as part of the bankruptcy estate. The bankruptcy office takes the necessary measures to convene the creditors for the initial creditor's meeting to nominate candidates to act as bankruptcy trustee. The responsibility of the trustee is to realize the assets of the company and to assure collection of the debts for the creditors. The trustee may also continue to operate the company and sell the business as a going concern.

14.6 Creditors Committee

[250] Within ten days from the declaration of ordinary liquidation announcement, the creditors are convened for the initial creditors' meeting which decides on the administration and liquidation of the bankruptcy estate. The main duty of creditors' meeting is to elect the bankruptcy trustee.

14.7 The Bankruptcy Trustee

[251] Pursuant to Article 223 of Enforcement and Bankruptcy Law, the bankruptcy trustee is a body of three members. The bankruptcy trustee is the legal representative of the bankruptcy estate. The main duties of the insolvency trustee are directing and liquidating the bankruptcy estate under the supervision of the enforcement office. Unless otherwise agreed by the creditors committee, members of the bankruptcy trustee represent the bankruptcy estate jointly. Members are liable for damages arising from their default actions. They cannot enter into a contract on their own. Enforcement office may raise claims against insolvency trustee's actions. In case of implementation of Turkish Criminal Code (Law No. 5237) ('Turkish Criminal Code'), members of insolvency trustee deemed as public officer.

14.8 Insolvency Register

[252] After liquidation process, bankruptcy trustee applies to the Commercial Register for deleting of bankrupt company's title from the Commercial Register and registration of the insolvency. Under Turkish legal system, there is no online access to insolvency register. To check a company's insolvency, it must be applied to the Commercial Register of company's head office stated with a petition including the company's full title and tax number.

14.9 Practical Problems

[253] The main problem in implementation of bankruptcy proceeding is the length of the terms. Collection and registry of receivables to bankruptcy estate, sale processes, liquidation, objections of creditors to other creditor's rankings are the main reasons for term extension. In practice, an ordinary bankruptcy proceeding takes approximately five or more years. Although Enforcement and Bankruptcy Law stipulates provisions for the protection of creditor against fraudulent bankruptcy or bad faith actions of debtor as selling out of the assets, in practice, it may not be possible to put in practice within these long terms.

14.10 Distribution of Assets: Priority Claims and Ranking

[254] After the liquidation process, collected cash is distributed to the creditors. The bankruptcy trustee issues a share table. Once the share table is issued; the order of collocation of the assets is normally as follows:

(i) The first step is taken by payment of public debts from the proceeds of liquidation of pledged assets.
(ii) As a second step, expenses related to storage and realization of pledged asset are allocated from the foreclosure amount.
(iii) Pledged receivables are paid from the remaining proceeds.

[255] After the satisfaction of pledgees, the remaining amount is added to bankruptcy estate and used for the satisfaction of ordinary creditors' claims. Ordinary creditors' claims are satisfied pursuant to the ranking listed below.

14.10.1 First Ranking

[256]

(i) Employment payments (included severance and notice payment) that accrued one year before the declaration of bankruptcy and included severance and notice payments of employers that are deserved by the termination of employment agreement by the reason of bankruptcy.
(ii) Employer's debts to associations which have been established with the aim of the supporting employees.
(iii) Alimony (*Nafaka*) debts hat accrued one year before the declaration of bankruptcy arisen from family law.

14.10.2 Second Ranking

[257]

(i) All receivables arise from guardian and ward relationship between debtor and creditor.

14.10.3 Third Ranking

(i) Receivables stipulated that they are privileged in special laws.

14.10.4 Fourth Ranking

(i) All other unprivileged receivables.

14.11 Concordat

[258] Enforcement and Bankruptcy Law provides 'concordat' as an option for restructuring the debtors' debts. Concordat proceedings may be initiated before the commercial court by the debtor or a creditor. The debtor is required to submit the following documents with its application for concordat:

(i) a preliminary concordat project that indicates the terms (i.e., proposed due dates and proposed amounts) under which the debtor will pay its debts, whether the debtor will sell its assets for those payments and the source of the funds (such as capital increase or borrowing) necessary for those payments;
(ii) documents that show financial situation of the debtor;
(iii) a table showing the creditors, the amount of their receivables and their priority;
(iv) a table comparing the amounts proposed by the debtor to be paid to the creditors in the preliminary concordat project, and the amounts that the creditors are likely to receive in the event of debtor's bankruptcy; and
(v) financial reports prepared by independent auditors, providing reasonable guarantee on the realization of the proposed payments in the preliminary concordat project.

[259] In case the concordat is requested by a creditor, the court will grant a reasonable period of time to the debtor for the preparation and filing of the documents above.

[260] Once the court determines that the application is complete, it appoints a concordat trustee, or a panel of trustees and grants a temporary concordat term of three months, which may be extended up to a total period of five months upon the debtor's or trustee's request.

[261] Within the temporary concordat term, the trustee reviews the preliminary concordat project and other documents and prepares a report for the court. If the report concludes that the concordat can be successfully completed and the court is convinced by the report, the court will grant a definitive concordat term of one year.

[262] During both the temporary and definitive concordat term, no execution proceedings can be enforced against the debtor and the existing execution proceedings are stopped, except for those relating to first-ranking receivables in bankruptcy proceedings (please *see* section 14.10.1 above). The creditors are invited to make their claims and to attend the creditors' meeting chaired by the trustee for the negotiation of the concordat project. At this meeting, the concordat project is required to be accepted by the majority of the creditors, who have registered themselves with the concordat trustee and whose receivables exceed half of the registered receivables or by a quarter of the registered creditors whose receivables exceed two-thirds of the registered receivables.

[263] Once the concordat project is accepted by the creditors as above, the trustee submits the concordat to the court for its approval within the definitive concordat term. The court will approve the concordat if it is convinced that the amount accepted under the concordat project is (i) higher than the amount that would possibly be collected by the creditors in bankruptcy proceedings, and (ii) proportional to the debtor's financial resources. In its approval decision, the court indicates the discount made by the creditors and the postponed due dates of the debts. The court's approval decision is binding for all creditors of the debtor, other than the receivables secured by a pledge, the first ranking receivables in the bankruptcy proceedings (please *see* section 14.10.1 above), the public receivables and the receivables that have occurred within the concordat term upon the permission of the trustee. In the event that the court rejects the concordat project, it declares the bankruptcy of the debtor.

15 LEGAL DUE DILIGENCE

15.1 General Introduction

[264] Purchasers normally carry out an investigation of the legal, financial, technological and environmental position of a target, as well as all relevant and related circumstances.

[265] A legal due diligence is generally conducted once the seller has committed to sell the target and the purchaser has expressed a strong interest in acquiring the target, often by signing either a 'letter of intent' or a 'memorandum of understanding', or has submitted a preliminary non-binding offer based on initial information provided by the seller and has, based on such offer, been granted exclusivity for negotiations with the seller for a certain period of time. At this stage, all relevant legal relationships, the validity of existing agreements and other legal matters must be clarified so that a final decision in respect of the acquisition may be taken.

15.2 Disclosure Restrictions

15.2.1 General

[266] Generally, even a majority shareholder is not entitled to instruct the target company to provide any information to a third party (a purchaser) for the purpose of a due diligence review, unless it is possible in accordance with the constitutional documents of the target company. Therefore, a due diligence process requires cooperation with the representatives of both the seller and the target company as the representatives of the target company are solely responsible for its business management and are obliged to act in the best interests of the target company, i.e., not the shareholders.

[267] In the course of a legal due diligence review, an investor may face restrictions on access to certain kinds of information and will commonly enter into a confidentiality agreement with the target company, regulating the access that is given.

15.2.2 Business Secrets

[268] A business secret includes any information, data, solution or fact the public disclosure of which as well as the receipt or use of which by unauthorized persons would breach or endanger the lawful financial, business or market interests of the holder of the business secret and for the preservation of which secret the holder of the business secret has taken the necessary steps to protect confidentiality. In the course of a due diligence, a reviewer will usually encounter business secrets of the target company, as well as business secrets of the entities in contractual (or other) relationships with the target company.

[269] It is within the sole discretion of the target company whether to disclose its business secrets to the prospective purchaser and, if so, to decide the terms and conditions for such disclosure.

[270] In relation to information classified as a business secret by third parties, unless the latter consents to data disclosure, the target company should ensure a level of protection corresponding to the scope of protection it owes to the respective third party.

15.2.3 Insider Information

[271] Publicly traded companies pose an additional challenge, as much information that a potential purchaser would be interested in reviewing may be qualified as insider information. Such information may generally be disclosed in a due diligence process provided that the recipient of such information is bound by a confidentiality agreement that specifically acknowledges that information to be provided may be insider information, and that the recipient undertakes to treat it accordingly.

15.2.4 Personal Data Protection

[272] Under Personal Data Protection Law, No. 6698 (*'Personal Data Protection Law'*), personal data means any data or information relating to an individual (identified or any individual who may be identifiable). This information will qualify as personal data regardless of the form in which it is expressed, or the medium which carries it, or by which order, on whose behalf, or by which interest that data is stored, regardless of the date of the data creation, the place where the data is stored, the method of obtaining the data, or other characteristics of the data.

[273] The target company's disclosure or transfer to the potential purchaser of any personal data must be made in accordance with Personal Data Protection Law. In principle, the target company should process (i.e., any operation on personal data, such as collection, recording, storage, retention, alteration, re-organization, disclosure, transfer, or classification) the personal data only upon the consent of the relevant individual. Personal Data Protection Law provides several exemptions for explicit consent requirement, including the cases where such a disclosure or transfer is expressly stipulated by the applicable legislation (e.g., court order), or it is necessary for the legitimate interests pursued by the processing party, provided that it shall not violate the fundamental rights and freedoms of the relevant individual. While the relevant legal rules provide for no general exception from the personal data protection obligations in the case of a due diligence process, it can be argued that the 'legitimate interest' exemption under Personal Data Protection Law is applicable in a due diligence process to the extent that the relevant data do not relate to the individual's fundamental rights and freedoms, such data are required for a correct valuation of the target company and the use of such data is proportionate to the purpose of valuation. In any event, the protection of personal data must be ensured by the target company and potentially other relevant parties (there are certain sectors where there are specific exceptions from the personal data protection obligations in the context of due diligence exercises, such as in the case of financial institutions).

15.2.5 Bank Secrecy

[274] Under the Banking Law, No. 5411 (*'Banking Law'*), all information, data, solution or fact, which are in possession of a bank and which are related to the person, data, pecuniary situation, business activities, ownership rights and business ties, the balance or traffic of the bank account, as well as the banking transactions and contracts of a client of a financial institution shall be handled as banking secrets. This applies to information concerning both natural and legal persons.

[275] Generally, a bank is prohibited from providing information that qualifies as banking secrets without its customer's consent, unless a specific exemption under the Banking Law, stipulates otherwise (e.g., a request made by the competent state authorities). For e.g., upon prior written approval of the board of directors of the respective bank, bank secrets may be disclosed to a shareholder of the respective bank, holding at least a qualified majority in the respective bank or also to prospective purchasers, including their auditors, legal advisors or other professionals of

such prospective purchaser, either intending to acquire at least a qualified majority stake in the respective bank or intending to acquire a business of the respective bank. Generally, such information is provided in aggregated form rather than in the form of information on individual bank clients.

[276] In addition to the above, the banks are subject to a stricter prohibition with respect to customer information. Unless there is a specific exemption under the Banking Law, the banks are prohibited from sharing any customer confidential information with third parties without the customer's express instruction, even if express consent was obtained in accordance with the Personal Data Protection Law.

15.2.6 Other Restrictions

[277] Confidentiality restrictions similar to those relating to banking secrets apply to specific regulated companies:

(i) insurance companies, where the insurance secrets of both individuals and corporate entities are protected pursuant to the Insurance Law, No. 5684;
(ii) investment firms, investment fund managers, venture capital fund managers, stock exchanges and clearing houses, where the securities of both individuals and corporate entities are protected pursuant to the CML.

[278] The CML imposes a general confidentiality duty on certain entities with respect to information that could potentially be important for the assessment of trends in the capital markets, or potentially harm an entity using the services rendered on the capital markets before such information is made public.

16 TAXATION

16.1 Turkish Tax System

[279] Currently, the Turkish tax system is primarily grouped around three basic systems of taxation.

16.1.1 Income Tax

[280] Income taxes in Turkey are based on the worldwide income of Turkish residents, foreigners residing in Turkey and international companies with a presence or activity in Turkey. Income of non-residents from commercial transactions, property and other activities in Turkey are also subject to Turkish income tax.

[281] Turkey has a network of double tax treaties which should be considered as well.

(i) Corporate Income Tax

[282] Turkish tax residents (companies with their registered seat or place of management or whose operations are centred and managed in Turkey) are taxed on their worldwide income. In Turkish tax legislation, they are described as full-liability taxpayers.

[283] The corporate tax rate for 2022 is 23% but tax incentives may provide reduced tax rates in certain cases.

[284] Where tax is paid abroad on foreign source income, a credit is applicable against the Turkish tax payable in respect of such income. Turkey has a network of tax treaties which facilitate international tax planning with a reasonably high degree of sophistication.

(ii) Personal Income Tax

[285] Personal income tax rates are progressive, ranging from approximately 15% to 40%. There are a limited number of basic personal deductions available. Foreigners resident in Turkey are subject to Turkish income tax on their worldwide income.

16.1.2 Excise Taxes

(i) Value Added Tax (VAT)

[286] The VAT is imposed on all goods delivered and services provided (including imported goods and services but excluding exports). The current general VAT rates are 1%, 8% and 18%, depending on the kind of goods and services.

(ii) Special Consumption Tax

[287] There are five categories of products which are subject to different rates of special consumption tax. These are (i) petroleum products, natural gas and derived solvents, (ii) automobiles and other vehicles, motorcycles, aeroplanes, helicopters and yachts, (iii) tobacco, tobacco products and alcoholic beverages, (iv) luxury goods, (v) white goods.

[288] Unlike the VAT that applies on every delivery, the special consumption tax applies only once upon the first sale.

(iii) Banking and Insurance Transactions Tax (BITT)

[289] Transactions made by banks or insurance companies are exempt from VAT but subject to BITT. The BITT is imposed on all types of payments received via banks and insurance companies where the banks and insurance companies derive income (e.g., interest income or similar fees). All types of transactions with banks and insurance companies except for financial leasing transactions are subject to BITT.

[290] The rates are as follows: (i) 1% for Interbank deposit accounts, Repurchase Agreement (REPO) transactions and sale of government bonds and treasury bills, (ii) 1% for foreign exchange transactions, (iii) 10% for consumer loans and (iv) 5% for other transactions.

(iv) Stamp Tax

[291] As a general rule, all documents listed in the Stamp Tax Law (e.g., agreements) are subject to stamp tax at a rate of 0.948% over the value stated in each original document. Stamp tax will accrue to the extent that (i) the relevant document is executed in Turkey or (ii) where the relevant document is not executed in Turkey, if (a) such document is submitted to the Turkish authorities (e.g., courts) or (b) such documents confer benefits in Turkey or (c) such documents are endorsed or transferred in Turkey. The cap for the stamp tax to be levied on each original document is currently TL4 814 234.

[292] However, documents (including loan and security documents) executed for loans extended by banks, foreign credit institutions or international finance institutions are exempt from the stamp tax. Both facility agreements and security documents securing loans from such lenders typically fall within the scope of exemption. In order to benefit from this exemption, the loan/funds should be disbursed to the accounts of the company in Turkey.

16.1.3 Capital Gains Tax

[293] Capital gains are normally considered to be ordinary income. However, capital gains derived from transfers of shares are exempt from income tax in certain cases.

[294] The withholding tax rate is reduced to 0% for capital gains derived by resident and non-resident individuals from the sale of shares traded on the Istanbul Stock Exchange. Capital gains derived from the disposal of shares that are not traded on the Istanbul Stock Exchange are subject to tax at the general progressive rates for ordinary income, provided that capital gains from the sale of shares of Turkish resident companies held for more than two years are exempt from tax.

16.2 Social Security Contribution

[295] Employers and employees pay monthly social security contributions at varying percentages calculated on gross salary, subject to upper and lower limits stated in the law. Employees pay contributions at a rate of 14%. Employers pay contributions at a rate of 20.5%, depending on the risk class of the business. The state treasury can reimburse 5% of the employers' contribution if certain conditions are fulfilled by the employer. The rates of unemployment insurance premiums are 1% for employees and 2% for employers.

16.3 Taxation Issues in Mergers and Acquisitions

16.3.1 Asset Purchase Transactions

[296] The parties in an asset purchase deal can recognize the goodwill and depreciate it over five years. Similarly, the tangible and intangible assets can be amortized.

(i) Purchase Price

[297] The transfer of assets must be at fair market value. Such transfer of assets must be documented properly in order to comply with transfer pricing requirements.

(ii) Tax Attributes

[298] Tax losses and incentives are not transferred to the buyer in an asset acquisition. The seller can use its existing tax losses and VAT credits against the taxable profits and VAT obligations resulting from the transfer of its assets.

[299] Generally, the potential tax liabilities of the seller should not be transferred to the buyer in an acquisition. There is one exception to this rule provided in the Law Regarding Collection of Public Receivables which provides that if the deal is structured to avoid the seller's tax liabilities (which is only possible in related party transactions), the tax office may set the transaction aside and pursue the assets.

(iii) Value-Added Tax

[300] Tax-free mergers which meet certain conditions in the Corporate Tax Law are exempt from VAT but taxable mergers are subject to 18% VAT. Transfers of real estate or shares/participation rights are exempted from VAT where they have been held by the seller for more than two years prior to the transfer.

[301] The sales of shares of a joint-stock company are exempt from VAT but such exemption applies to limited liability companies only if the participation has been held for at least two years. No VAT obligation applies in cases of sales of shares by individuals.

(iv) Transfer Taxes

[302] As provided in section 16.1.2 'Stamp Tax' above, certain documents executed in Turkey are subject to stamp tax, including merger agreements. Documents for (i) tax-free mergers and (ii) the sale of real estate property or shares/participation rights held by a company for more than two years are exempted from stamp tax.

16.3.2 Share Purchase Transactions

[303] The acquisition of shares by a foreign entity does not result in immediate Turkish income tax obligations. In case of an acquisition made through a Turkish branch or subsidiary, the goodwill which is included in the share price cannot be recognized for amortization.

[304] A change in shareholders does not affect the tax attributes of the target company.

(i) Tax Indemnities and Warranties

[305] In a share deal, the effective cost of meeting tax obligations of the target company is acquired by the buyer. It is customary for a buyer to require tax indemnities and warranties.

(ii) Tax Losses

[306] Tax losses can be carried forward for five years and carryback is not possible. In case of a tax-free merger, the merged entity can use the tax losses of the merging entity.

(iii) Transfer Taxes

[307] As a result of a specific exemption of the Corporate Tax Law, the documents relating to transfers of shares of Turkish companies which have been held for at least two years are exempt from capital gains tax.

(iv) Tax Clearances

[308] The Turkish authorities do not provide tax clearances regarding the tax status of a company; however, they do provide an unofficial statement indicating the reported but unpaid tax obligations of the company, if any. As such statements are not completely reliable, it is advisable to conduct tax due diligence in the course of a merger or acquisition.

16.3.3 Structuring of the Acquisition

(i) Local Holding Company

[309] Both joint-stock companies and limited liability companies are frequently used where a local holding company is required.

(ii) Foreign Parent Company

[310] If the foreign investor chooses to make the acquisition itself, or through a foreign holding company, withholding tax on interest and dividend payments to such company will apply.

(iii) Local Branch

[311] Using a branch of a foreign company to acquire or hold shares of a Turkish target company is not generally advisable because:

- dividends paid by the Turkish target to the branch of the foreign entity will be taxable and the participation exemption would not apply;
- all profits and dividends from the branch to the foreign parent company would be subject to withholding tax; and

- on an exit scenario, as the branch cannot be separately transferred to a third party, structuring options such as mergers are not as flexible as might be preferred.

(iv) Joint Venture

[312] A joint venture may be established between a Turkish company and one or more Turkish or foreign entities. This joint venture can take an incorporated form under a joint-stock company or limited liability company form and is subject to the same tax treatment as other Turkish companies.

16.3.4 Acquisition Financing

[313]

(i) A purchaser needs to consider how to fund the acquisition vehicle – by debt or equity. Since hybrid financing instruments are not recognized for tax purposes in Turkey, the legal definition must be followed when financing the structure as debt or equity.
(ii) There is no limit on the amount of debt that can be put into a Turkish company and no general limitation on the deductibility of interest, subject to thin capitalization rules, transfer pricing rules and interest incurred on share acquisitions.
(iii) Equity injections are subject to a competition board fee of 0.04%. No other taxes and duties are levied on equity funding.
(iv) Turkish Corporate Tax Law allows for tax-free mergers, demergers and share swaps, provided that certain procedural obligations are met.

16.3.5 Other Considerations

[314]

(i) Gains of non-residents except where the non-resident has a permanent establishment or a permanent representative in Turkey are subject to tax as a limited taxpayer. Specific rules apply with respect to capital gains derived from disposal of shares by a non-resident.
(ii) The seller is liable for tax on gains on the sale of the assets of a business and shares.

17 ACCOUNTING TREATMENT

17.1 Accounting Obligations

[315] The TCC provides that legal entities and natural persons acting as sole traders (i.e., all companies) which meet the criteria set out below, must comply with

Turkish Financial Reporting Standards (TFRS) as prepared by Turkish Accounting Standards Board (TASB). The TFRS is the translation of International Financial Reporting Standards (IFRS). The TCC requires that all companies must comply with the TFRS in their bookkeeping and financial reporting as of 1 January 2013.

[316] All publicly traded companies are required to use IFRS in their consolidated financial statements. All other companies are required to follow the methods stipulated in the Tax Procedure Law No. 213 (TPL).

[317] Statutory audit: All companies that meet any two of the following three criteria for two consecutive years are bound to perform a statutory audit for 2022:

(i) if the total assets of the company are equal to or more than TL35 m;
(ii) if the revenue of the company is equal to or more than TL70 m; or
(iii) if the average number of employees of the company is 175 or more.

[318] Companies whose capital market instruments are not traded in stock market or an organized market but which are deemed publicly held under the CML that meet any two of the following three criteria for two consecutive years are bound to perform a statutory audit for 2022:

(i) if the total assets of the company are equal to or more than TL15 m;
(ii) if the revenue of the company is equal to or more than TL20 m; or
(iii) if the average number of employees of the company is fifty or more.

[319] Companies (i) whose at least 50% of the issued capital is owned by municipalities; (ii) whose at least 25% of the issued capital is owned directly or indirectly by public, professional organizations, labour unions, associations, foundations, cooperatives and their superior organization; (iii) which are licensed by Energy Market Regulatory Agency; (iv) which are transferred to Saving Deposit Insurance Fund or its affiliates; (v) which are under the supervision of Information and Technology and Communication Authority; and (vi) public economic enterprises, that meet any two of the following three criteria for two consecutive years are bound to perform a statutory audit for 2022:

(i) if the total assets of the company are equal to or more than TL30 m;
(ii) if the revenue of the company is equal to or more than TL40 m; or
(iii) if the average number of employees of the company is 125 or more.

17.2 The Tax Procedure Law

[320] The TPL does not regulate consolidation, therefore, all companies reporting in accordance with this law must prepare stand-alone financial statements. Other notable features of the TPL include:

- TPL does not permit any recognition of goodwill.
- TPL accounting principles recognize value on the basis of carrying values and not fair value.

- In the context of acquisitions, the TPL recognizes the effective date of an acquisition as the acquisition is registered with the Commercial Register.
- Upon an acquisition, profits of the target company(ies) are included within the acquiring company's profit and loss account.

www.ingramcontent.com/pod-product-compliance
Ingram Content Group UK Ltd.
Pitfield, Milton Keynes, MK11 3LW, UK
UKHW020151290926
15471UKWH00004B/814

9 789403 528564